MY FAVOURITE HYMN

MY FAVOURITE
FAVOURITE
Hymn

COMPILED BY GRAHAM FERGUSON LACEY

Sold in aid of the British Red Cross

Robson Books

Dedicated To 'HIM' Without Whom There Would Be No 'Hymn'

First published in Great Britain in 1999 by Robson Books, 10 Blenheim Court, Brewery Road, London N7 9NT

A member of the Chrysalis Group plc

Compilation copyright © Graham Ferguson Lacey 1999
Photographs © Gemma Levine, except p. 13 – photograph by Anthony Crickmay/courtesy of Camera Press

A minimum of £3.00 per book sold is paid to Britcross Limited which covenants all its taxable profits to The British Red Cross Society (a registered charity number 220949)

British Library Cataloguing in Publication Data
A catalogue record for this title is available from the British Library

ISBN 1 86105 297 9

Typeset by SX Composing DTP, Rayleigh, Essex
Printed and bound in Spain by Bookprint S.L., Barcelona

C O N T E N T S

Acknowledgements

This book would not have been possible without the encouragement of Kay Talbot, the extreme patience and hard work of my executive assistants, Katrina Shallcross and Lesley Dorsett, the enthusiastic support of Jeremy Robson and his editors, Anthea Matthison and Lorna Russell, the copyright work of Jill Kendrick and Michael Mizen, and the contributions that were facilitated by Anthony Cordle, Geoffrey Gelardi, Gemma Levine, Lord Reading and Eunice Salmond. Special thanks to John Gray of the British Red Cross.

FOREWORD

HRH Prince Michael of Kent

My Favourite Hymn has managed to combine the marvelous language of some of our best loved hymns with the memories of their music. The result is a collection of personal choices, together with the reason for them, from one hundred people across the spectrum of national life in Britain. I am very grateful to them for taking the time to contribute to this book for the benefit of the British Red Cross.

The compiler, Graham Ferguson Lacey, in dreaming up this book and sponsoring it, has created a fundraising opportunity that demonstrates the breadth of the Red Cross and Red Crescent movement by combining the thoughts of followers of every faith.

I am delighted to wish this charming book every success.

PREFACE

Graham Ferguson Lacey

Hymn singing is one of the most popular and best loved parts of our musical heritage. The alliance of melody, harmony and rhythm with words that touch our deepest emotions, triggering images and feelings of moments passed and our dreams yet to be, makes the great hymns of Christendom more memorable than any music.

The tradition goes back many centuries – indeed millennia – to the chanting of psalms. From then until now there has been an astonishing outpouring of hymns from every denomination of the Christian church, from many different countries and many different ethnic traditions.

In our culture, hymns learnt at Sunday School or secular school, sung at weddings, christenings, funerals or celebrations have long encapsulated special memories, some of which are happy, some sad, but nevertheless memories that tug at our emotions and are an integral part of the rich tapestry of our lives.

My Favourite Hymn was conceived as an opportunity to bring together a collection of our nation's favourite hymns by asking the same two questions of 100 personalities from right across the spectrum of our society: 'What is your favourite hymn' and 'Why?'

This book incorporates those answers. Some of those asked replied with poems or book quotations; these have been excluded, for perhaps one day there will be *My Favourite Poem*. However, the book contains choices right across the Christian denominations, as well as the Jewish and Muslim

faiths. To each who have contributed - my sincerest thanks. To those who declined because they were atheists or agnostics – my respect. And to those who submitted their hymn choice and reason but were unable to be photographed by the book's retained photographer, I am pleased that we have been able to include your contribution nevertheless.

My favourite hymn is: 'Face to face with Christ My Saviour'. It was a favourite of my older brother, Adrian, who had a lifetime of chronic asthma, leading to his untimely death at the age of 23, and was part of the rich and conclusive influence he had in introducing me to a personal faith in Jesus Christ with all of its marvellous attendant promises.

This book, in reflecting the hymn choices of participants that are representative of almost every main religious denomination, and none, will contribute to the British Red Cross Disaster Appeal about £3 for each copy sold. The British Red Cross, with its respected neutrality and earned respect, is a most deserving and appropriate beneficiary.

The new millennium is saluted appropriately by *My Favourite Hymn* and the purchase of this book has been designed to bless the participants, the purchasers and the British Red Cross. To all of you – thank you.

FACE TO FACE WITH CHRIST MY SAVIOUR

Face to face with Christ my Saviour,
Face to face – what will it be?
When with rapture I behold Him,
Jesus Christ who died for me.
Face to face shall I behold Him,
Far beyond the starry sky;
Face to face in all His glory,
I shall see Him by and by!

Only faintly now I see Him,
With the darkling veil between,
But a blessed day is coming,
When His glory shall be seen.
Face to face . . .

What rejoicing in His presence,
When are banished grief and pain;
When the crooked ways are straightened
And the dark things shall be plain
Face to face . . .

Face to face! O blissful moment!
Face to face – to see and know!
Face to face with my Redeemer,
Jesus Christ who loves me so.
Face to face . . .

MRS FRANK A BRECK

HRH PRINCESS ALEXANDRA

Deputy President, British Red Cross

WHEN I SURVEY THE WONDROUS CROSS

When I survey the wondrous cross,
on which the Prince of glory died,
my richest gain I count but loss,
and pour contempt on all my pride.

Forbid it, Lord, that I should boast
save in the death of Christ my God;
all the vain things that charm me most,
I sacrifice them to His blood.

See from His head, His hands, His feet,
sorrow and love flow mingled down;
did e'er such love and sorrow meet,
or thorns compose so rich a crown?

Were the whole realm of nature mine,
that were a present far too small;
love so amazing, so divine,
demands my soul, my life, my all.

ISAAC WATTS (1674–1748)

Photograph: Anthony Crickmay/courtesy of Camera Press

TONY ADAMS

Footballer

'Morning Has Broken' simply reminds me of my childhood days. When at school we would sing this hymn.

MORNING HAS BROKEN

Morning has broken
like the first morning;
blackbird has spoken
like the first bird.
Praise for the singing!
Praise for the morning!
Praise for them, springing
fresh from the Word!

Sweet the rain's new fall
sunlit from heaven,
like the first dewfall
on the first grass.
Praise for the sweetness
of the wet garden,
sprung in completeness
where His feet pass.

Mine is the sunlight!
Mine is the morning
born of the one light
Eden saw play!
Praise with elation,
praise every morning,
God's re-creation
of the new day!

ELEANOR FARJEON (1881–1965)

From *The Children's Bells* published by Oxford University Press.

KRISS AKABUSI

Television Personality and Athlete

My favourite hymn is 'There Is A Green Hill Far Away'. Although I could have chosen any one of a number of hymns that bring back memories of childhood, this one in particular brings back vivid memories of singing in school assembly with my friends. Sometimes I would just pretend to be singing – sometimes I would sing really loud! But all the time, I would have pictures in my mind of a God who suffered for us, a God who loved us and a God who cared for us. Also, it made me feel a sense of unity with those around me, a sense of nationality and a sense of belonging to a family. Isn't it a pity that wars seem to contradict these sentiments?

THERE IS A GREEN HILL FAR AWAY

There is a green hill far away,
Without a city wall,
Where the dear Lord was crucified,
Who died to save us all.

We may not know, we cannot tell
What pains He had to bear;
But we believe it was for us
He hung and suffered there.

He died that we might be forgiven,
He died to make us good,
That we might go at last to heaven,
Saved by His precious blood.

There was no other good enough
To pay the price of sin;
He only could unlock the gate
Of heaven, and let us in.

Oh, dearly, dearly has He loved!
And we must love Him too;
And trust in His redeeming blood,
And try His works to do.

C F ALEXANDER (1818–91)

LORD DAVID ALTON

Director of The Foundation for Citizenship,
Liverpool John Moores University

At the time I was promoting my Bill to save the lives of unborn children, Graham Kendrick wrote his hymn 'Who Can Sound The Depths Of Sorrow'. It was sung at the Manchester Free Trade Hall and the Royal Albert Hall by thousands of supporters while millions of white petals, representing the five million babies aborted over the past thirty years, drifted from the roof. It was extremely poignant and moving.

This hymn is about all heartbreaking situations and reminds us that Christ himself stands at the heart of the brokenness of our lives.

WHO CAN SOUND THE DEPTHS OF SORROW

Who can sound the depths of sorrow
in the Father heart of God,
for the children we've rejected,
for the lives so deeply scarred?
And each light that we've extinguished
has brought darkness to our land:
upon the nation, upon the nation
have mercy Lord!

We have scorned the truth You gave us,
we have bowed to other lords,
we have sacrificed the children
on the altars of our gods.
O let truth again shine on us,
let Your holy fear descend:
upon the nation, upon the nation
have mercy Lord!

Who can sound the depths of mercy
in the Father heart of God?
For there is a Man of sorrows
who for sinners shed His blood.
He can heal the wounds of nations,
He can wash the guilty clean:
because of Jesus, because of Jesus,
have mercy Lord!

GRAHAM KENDRICK (b. 1950)

PADDY ASHDOWN

MP and Former Leader of the Liberal Democrats

I think if I was asked my favourite hymn I would have to say 'I Vow To Thee My Country'. As you may know, the tune is from Holst's *Planets* 'Venus'. I understand that Holst was one day wandering through London (Charing Cross Road, I think) and saw a poem in a shop window which he discovered fitted precisely the theme for 'Venus'.

The hymn is often used rather jingoistically at Remembrance Day services etc. But it is, in my view, not jingoistic at all when you look at it and a very remarkable evocation of that spirit of decency and spiritual commitment which can also exist in the middle of the ravages of war.

I VOW TO THEE MY COUNTRY

I vow to thee my country,
all earthly things above,
entire and whole and perfect,
the service of my love:
the love that asks no questions,
the love that stands the test,
that lays upon the altar
the dearest and the best;
the love that never falters,
the love that pays the price,
the love that makes undaunted
the final sacrifice.

And there's another country,
I've heard of long ago,
most dear to them that love her,
most great to them that know;
we may not count her armies,
we may not see her King;
her fortress is a faithful heart,
her pride is suffering;
and soul by soul and silently
her shining bounds increase,
and her ways are ways of gentleness
and all her paths are peace.

CECIL SPRING-RICE (1859–1918)

ROWAN ATKINSON

Comedy Actor

"My personal favourite is one whose first line is 'The day Thou gavest, Lord, is ended' to the tune of St Clement. Evensong has always been my favourite service of the Church of England, because the evening always seems to be the most peaceful and spiritually inspiring time and the tune which normally accompanies these words is extremely moving. "

THE DAY THOU GAVEST

The day Thou gavest, Lord, is
ended,
The darkness falls at Thy behest;
To Thee our morning hymns
ascended,
Thy praise shall sanctify our rest.

We thank Thee that Thy church
unsleeping,
While earth rolls onward into light,
Through all the world her watch is
keeping,
And rests not now by day or night.

As o'er each continent and island
The dawn leads on another day,
The voice of prayer is never silent,
Nor dies the strain of praise away.

The sun that bids us rest is waking
Our brethren 'neath the western
sky,
And hour by hour fresh lips are
making
Thy wondrous doings heard on
high.

So be it, Lord; Thy throne shall never,
Like earth's proud empires, pass
away;
Thy kingdom stands, and grows for
ever,
Till all Thy creatures own Thy
sway.

JOHN ELLERTON (1826–93)

PAM AYRES

Poet

My favourite hymn is 'Dear Lord And Father Of Mankind'. This hymn brings back lots of vivid and happy images of my village childhood. It reminds me of my small village primary school in Stanford-in-the-Vale where I was brought up and lived until I was eighteen. I can remember singing it, standing on the school's wooden floorboards, surrounded by my friends and family (I am one of six brothers and sisters), feeling very safe and secure. I can still see Miss Perkins, the head teacher, who was immensely tall and who wore grey suede sandals. I also enjoy the range of the hymn; it always seems to me to be a good hymn that you can sing with gusto.

DEAR LORD AND FATHER OF MANKIND

Dear Lord and Father of mankind,
forgive our foolish ways;
re-clothe us in our rightful mind;
in purer lives Thy service find,
in deeper reverence, praise.

In simple trust like theirs who heard,
beside the Syrian sea,
the gracious calling of the Lord,
let us, like them, without a word
rise up and follow Thee.

O Sabbath rest by Galilee!
O calm of hills above,
where Jesus knelt to share with Thee
the silence of eternity,
interpreted by love!

With that deep hush subduing all,
our words and works that drown,
the tender whisper of Thy call,
as noiseless let Thy blessing fall,
as fell Thy manna down.

Drop Thy still dews of quietness,
till all our strivings cease;
take from our souls the strain and stress,
and let our ordered lives confess
the beauty of Thy peace.

Breathe through the heats of our desire
Thy coolness and Thy balm;
let sense be dumb, let flesh retire;
speak through the earthquake, wind, and fire,
O still small voice of calm!

J G WHITTIER (1807–92)

Repton

C. H. H. PARRY (1848–1918)
from a song in his oratorio *Judith*

DR ZAKI BADAWI

Principal Professor of the Muslim College

"'The Prayer Of The Oppressed' is based on a supplication by the Prophet Muhammad at a time when the people of the town of Taif in Arabia rejected him and pursued him out of the town throwing stones at him and forcing him to take refuge in an orchard where he was cared for by a Christian slave.

I repeat this prayer every time I face a crisis."

THE PRAYER OF THE OPPRESSED

Lord I place before You my weakness and utter vulnerability and the lowly status in the eyes of the people. You are the Lord of the oppressed and You are my Lord. To whom do you entrust my fate? To an enemy who will ill-treat me or to a stranger who will look upon me with disdain? If it should be Your Will I shall submit without complaint. My entire being is devoted to seeking Your Pleasure. You are the Master of the World and the Hereafter. You are the most Merciful and Compassionate. To You alone we turn for succour and You alone we worship. Glory and praise are Yours alone.

MUSLIM PRAYER

RONNIE BARKER

Comedy Actor

I'm not, I fear, a believer, but I *love* hymns. As a boy, I was in the church choir and when my voice broke I began to learn the bass harmonies. The hymn that I have chosen – 'Praise To The Holiest In The Height' – captured me because of the wonderful rising bass harmonies, especially in the third line.

PRAISE TO THE HOLIEST IN THE HEIGHT

Praise to the Holiest in the height,
and in the depth be praise;
in all His words most wonderful;
most sure in all His ways.

O loving wisdom of our God!
when all was sin and shame,
a second Adam to the fight,
and to the rescue came.

O wisest love! that flesh and blood
which did in Adam fail,
should strive afresh against the foe,
should strive and should prevail.

And that a higher gift than grace
should flesh and blood refine,
God's presence, and His very self
and essence all-divine.

O generous love! that He, who smote
in Man for man the foe,
the double agony in Man
for man should undergo.

And in the garden secretly,
and on the cross on high,
should teach His brethren, and inspire
to suffer and to die.

Praise to the Holiest in the height
and in the depth be praise:
in all His words most wonderful;
most sure in all His ways.

JOHN HENRY NEWMAN (1801–90)

MARTIN BELL

MP and Journalist

My favourite hymn is hardly an original one, but near the top of everyone's list, 'All People That On Earth Do Dwell'.

It expresses for me the enduring consolations and truths of religion. It is popular with the armed services, among whom I have spent a great deal of my professional life. They sing it at their remembrance services, and cherish it, for its words as much as its music. It has meant a great deal to me in dangerous places and difficult times.

ALL PEOPLE THAT ON EARTH DO DWELL

All people that on earth do dwell,
Sing to the Lord with cheerful voice;
Him serve with mirth,
His praise forth tell;
come ye before Him and rejoice.

The Lord, ye know, is God indeed:
without our aid He did us make:
we are His folk, He doth us feed;
and for His sheep He doth us take.

O enter then His gates with praise,
approach with joy His courts unto;
praise, laud, and bless His name always,
for it is seemly so to do.

For why? The Lord our God is good;
His mercy is for ever sure;
His truth at all times firmly stood,
and shall from age to age endure.

W KETHE (d. 1954)

PSALM 100

Old Hundredth   LM

Later form of melody in the *Genevan Psalter*, 1551

31

DAVID BELLAMY

Broadcaster and Botanist

My favourite hymn is 'All Things Bright And Beautiful'.

For obvious reasons, it was the first hymn I sang at Sunday school, now 62 years ago, and certainly is part of the reason that I am a botanist and a campaigner for the preservation of the living world.

ALL THINGS BRIGHT AND BEAUTIFUL

All things bright and beautiful,
all creatures great and small,
all things wise and wonderful,
the Lord God made them all.

Each little flower that opens,
each little bird that sings,
He made their glowing colours,
He made their tiny wings.
All things bright . . .

The purple-headed mountain,
the river running by,
the sunset, and the morning
that brightens up the sky;
All things bright . . .

The cold wind in the winter,
the pleasant summer sun,
the ripe fruits in the garden,
He made them every one.
All things bright . . .

He gave us eyes to see them,
and lips that we might tell
how great is God almighty,
who has made all things well.
All things bright . . .

C F ALEXANDER (1818–95)

MARY BERRY

Cookery Writer and Broadcaster

"'Onward, Christian Soldiers' was composed by Arthur Sullivan who was a frequent visitor when Sir George Grove lived here at Watercroft and for this reason I have a great affection for this hymn. We sing it at family weddings and funerals."

ONWARD, CHRISTIAN SOLDIERS

Onward, Christian soldiers,
marching as to war,
with the cross of Jesus going on before.
Christ the royal Master
leads against the foe;
forward into battle, see, His banners go!
Onward, Christian soldiers,
marching as to war,
with the cross of Jesus going on before.

At the name of Jesus
Satan's legions flee;
on then, Christian soldiers,
on to victory.
Hell's foundations quiver
at the shout of praise;
brothers, lift your voices,
loud your anthems raise.
Onward, Christian soldiers . . .

Like a mighty army
moves the Church of God;
brothers, we are treading
where the saints have trod;
we are not divided, all one body we,
one in hope and calling, one in charity.
Onward, Christian soldiers . . .

Onward, then, ye people,
join our happy throng,
blend with ours your voices
in the triumph song;
glory, praise and honour
unto Christ the King;
This through countless ages
men and angels sing.
Onward, Christian soldiers . . .

SABINE BARING-GOULD (1834–1924)

TONY BLAIR

Prime Minister

> "The hymn 'Jerusalem' has been chosen by the Prime Minister because it is symbolic of his feelings for New Labour."

JERUSALEM

And did those feet in ancient time
Walk upon England's mountains green?
And was the Holy Lamb of God
On England's pleasant pastures seen?
And did the countenance divine
Shine forth upon our clouded hills?
And was Jerusalem builded here
Among these dark satanic mills?

Bring me my bow of burning gold!
Bring me my arrows of desire!
Bring me my spear! O clouds, unfold!
Bring me my chariot of fire!
I will not cease from mental fight,
Nor shall my sword sleep in my hand,
Till we have built Jerusalem
In England's green and pleasant land.

WILLIAM BLAKE (1757–1827)

CHERIE BOOTH

Barrister QC

"Jessie Norman sang 'Amazing Grace' at the White House, at the fiftieth anniversary of NATO."

AMAZING GRACE

Amazing grace –
how sweet the sound –
that saved a wretch like me!
I once was lost, but now am found,
was blind, but now I see.

'Twas grace that taught my heart
to fear,
and grace my fears relieved;
how precious did that grace appear
the hour I first believed.

Through many dangers,
toils and snares,
I have already come;
'tis grace hath brought me safe thus far,
and grace will lead me home.

When we've been there
ten thousand years
bright shining as the sun,
we've no less days to sing God's praise
than when we've first begun.

JOHN NEWTON (1725–1807)
LAST VERSE: JOHN REES (1828–1900)

BETTY BOOTHROYD

Speaker of the House of Commons

"My favourite hymn is 'Morning Has Broken' because it is bright and cheerful and it makes you think you are lucky to be alive at the beginning of a new day."

MORNING HAS BROKEN

Morning has broken
like the first morning;
blackbird has spoken
like the first bird.
Praise for the singing!
Praise for the morning!
Praise for them, springing
fresh from the Word!

Sweet the rain's new fall
sunlit from heaven,
like the first dewfall
on the first grass.
Praise for the sweetness
of the wet garden,
sprung in completeness
where His feet pass.

Mine is the sunlight!
Mine is the morning
born of the one light
Eden saw play!
Praise with elation,
praise every morning,
God's re-creation
of the new day!

ELEANOR FARJEON (1881–1965)

From *The Children's Bells* published by Oxford University Press.

RICHARD BRANSON

Entrepreneur

"My favourite hymn is 'The Holly And The Ivy' and the reason being that it is the only song I can remember the words to!"

THE HOLLY AND THE IVY

The holly and the ivy,
when they are both full grown,
of all the trees that are in the wood
the holly bears the crown.
The rising of the sun,
and the running of the deer,
the playing of the merry organ,
sweet singing in the choir.

The holly bears a blossom,
white as the lily flow'r,
and Mary bore sweet Jesus Christ
to be our sweet Saviour.

The holly bears a berry,
as red as any blood,
and Mary bore sweet Jesus Christ
to do poor sinners good.

The holly bears a prickle,
as sharp as any thorn,
and Mary bore sweet Jesus Christ
on Christmas day in the morn.

TRADITIONAL

LESLIE BRICUSSE

Lyricist

For me the best and most inspirational of all hymns, the melody for 'Jerusalem' was composed by Sir Charles Hubert Parry in 1916 – more than a century after that remarkable mystic poet-illustrator and visionary, William Blake, created the now-famous words as part of his epic poem 'Milton' (1804–08). Two far distant eras combined to produce a musical marriage made in Heaven. I hope it is not too irreverent to say that 'Jerusalem' is a veritable show-stopper.

Throughout my life I have always been moved and uplifted whenever I have heard 'Jerusalem', and never more than when I first saw the film *Chariots of Fire* in 1981, where the film's composer Vangelis used it so brilliantly to celebrate the triumphant homecoming of Britain's victorious athletes after the 1924 Paris Olympiad.

The story concerned itself mainly with the different paths to Olympic glory taken by two violently contrasted athletes, Harold Abrahams and Eric Liddell – the ruthless and arrogant ambition of one, and the inspired and unshakeable faith of the other. Both those powerful motivating ingredients are to be found in the words and the music of 'Jerusalem'.

My awareness was heightened still more by the fact that in my years at Cains College, Cambridge, I had occupied the very rooms that, 35 years before, had accommodated and nurtured Harold Abraham's will to succeed. And it is that unique clarion call of 'Jerusalem' – willing us to action and achievement – that will for ever give it its honoured place in my abiding musical affections.

*The words to 'Jerusalem' appear on page 36.

PAUL BURRELL

Humanitarian

'Make Me A Channel Of Your Peace' has to be my favourite hymn. These words bring comfort to so many and are everything which we could wish to aspire to.

Two years after that dreadful tragedy [the death of the Princess of Wales], I can still remember singing these words in Westminster Abbey and vividly remember thinking that these were the hopes, the dreams and the ideals of a uniquely inspirational and irreplaceable human being. Her mission in life was to bring hope to those who had been forgotten and to shine that much needed light into the dark corners of the world.

During the same year I was asked to accept a cheque on behalf of the Memorial Fund, at a primary school in Warrington. Faced by two hundred bright, shiny faces I was moved again by the same words. Angelic voices accompanied by recorders and tambourines reminded me that these children were the hope for the future. How could anyone not appreciate such purity and innocence?

MAKE ME A CHANNEL OF YOUR PEACE

Make me a channel of your peace
Where there is hatred, let me bring your love
Where there is injury, your pardon, Lord
And where there's doubt, truth faith in you

Make me a channel of your peace
Where there's despair in life, let me bring hope
Where there is darkness only light,
And where there's sadness ever joy

Oh, Master, grant that I may never seek
So much to be consoled as to console
To be understood as to understand
To be loved, as to love, with all my soul

Make me a channel of your peace
It is pardoning that we are pardoned
In giving to all men, that we receive
And in dying that we're born to eternal life

SEBASTIAN TEMPLE (b. 1928)
BASED ON A PRAYER OF ST FRANCIS OF ASSISI
DEDICATED TO MRS FRANCIS TRACY

LAVINIA BYRNE

Religious Broadcaster

" I can remember when I first sang 'Soul Of My Saviour'. I had golden curly hair and stood on the seat in church facing backwards towards the choir. I must have been six years old. I belted it out, believed in it fervently because it's all about salvation. Now I want to have it at my funeral. "

SOUL OF MY SAVIOUR

Soul of my saviour, sanctify my breast,
body of Christ, be thou my saving guest,
blood of my saviour, bathe me in thy tide,
wash me with water flowing from thy side.

Strength and protection may thy passion be,
O blessed Jesu, hear and answer me;
deep in thy wounds, Lord, hide and shelter me,
so shall I never, never part from thee.

Guard and defend me from the foe malign,
in death's dread moments make me only thine;
call me and bid me come to thee on high
where I may praise thee with thy saints for ay.

LATIN, 14TH CENTURY TRANS. ANON

SIMON CALLOW

Actor

I was brought up a Roman Catholic. There's a perfectly decent tradition of English Catholic hymns, but nothing quite to compare with the majestic splendour of 'Rock Of Ages' or 'Abide With Me', or the fervour of the Wesleyan oeuvre. One, however, always stirred me, and it's the only one I can remember today. I've no idea who wrote the noble tune, but the words were by G K Chesterton, a hero of mine then and now. I have long ceased to believe in any celestial God (though firmly believing in the God within each of us), but the hymn's sentiments are as applicable on the brink of the third millennium as they were on the brink of the twentieth century when GKC was writing.

O GOD OF EARTH AND ALTAR

O God of earth and altar,
Bow down and hear our cry,
Our earthly rulers falter,
Our people drift and die;
The walls of gold entomb us,
The swords of scorn divide,
Take not thy thunder from us,
But take away our pride.

From all that terror teaches,
From lies of tongue and pen,
From all the easy speeches
That comfort cruel men,
From sale and profanation
Of honour and the sword,
From sleep and from damnation,
Deliver us, good Lord!

Tie in a living tether
The prince and priest and thrall,
Bind all our lives together,
Smite us and save us all;
In ire and exultation
Aflame with faith, and free,
Lift up a living nation,
A single sword to thee.

G K CHESTERTON (1874–1936)

By permission of Oxford University Press.

GEORGE CAREY

Archbishop of Canterbury

My wife, Eileen, and I originally chose 'O Praise Ye The Lord' for our wedding. We have sung it at every great moment of our lives since – at the baptism of our children; when I became Vicar of St Nicholas' Durham; when I was installed as Principal of Trinity College, Bristol; and when I was consecrated Bishop and later Archbishop. Our children have had it as their wedding hymn, and it will be sung at my funeral, although I hope that will not be for some time yet!

It is a great hymn of praise. It outlines the wonderful story of salvation and lifts our eyes to the promise of God – that he is Creator, Friend and Lover. He is there at our beginning and will be there when we pass from this life into his arms. For me, it puts everything into perspective.

O PRAISE YE THE LORD

O praise ye the Lord!
praise Him in the height;
rejoice in His word,
ye angels of light;
ye heavens adore Him
by whom ye were made,
and worship before Him,
in brightness arrayed.

O praise ye the Lord!
praise Him upon earth,
in tuneful accord,
ye sons of new birth;
praise Him who has brought you
His grace from above,
praise Him who has taught you
to sing of His love.

O praise ye the Lord!
all things that give sound;
each jubilant chord,
re-echo around;
loud organs, His glory
forth tell in deep tone,
and sweet harp, the story
of what He has done.

O praise ye the Lord!
thanksgiving and song
to Him be outpoured
all ages along:
for love in creation,
for heaven restored,
for grace of salvation,
O praise ye the Lord!

H W BAKER (1821–77)

FIONA CASTLE

Christian Author

I first heard 'For The Joys And For The Sorrows' being sung at Spring Harvest 1995, shortly after my husband, Roy, had died. It had a huge impact on me. It expresses in a beautiful way the value of the relationship we can have with Jesus. He is with us to help us in every circumstance of our lives. What an offer! I can't understand why anyone would refuse! I have proved Jesus to be faithful.

Graham Kendrick has written some wonderful hymns and will surely go down in history as the greatest hymn-writer of this century. I am grateful to him for providing me with so many songs to worship the Lord in so many different ways.

FOR THE JOYS AND FOR THE SORROWS

For the joys and for the sorrows,
The best and worst of times;
For this moment, for tomorrow,
For all that lies behind.
Fears that crowd around me;
For the failure of my plans;
For the dreams of all I hope to be,
The truth of what I am –

For the tears that flow in secret
In the broken times;
For the moments of elation,
Or the troubled mind;
For all the disappointments
Or the sting of old regrets;
All my prayers and longings
That seem unanswered yet –

For the weakness of my body,
The burdens of each day;
For the nights of doubt and worry
When sleep has fled away;
Needing reassurance
And the will to start again,
A steely-eyed endurance,
The strength to fight and win –

For this I have Jesus,
For this I have Jesus,
For this I have Jesus,
I have Jesus.

GRAHAM KENDRICK (b. 1950)

BARONESS LYNDA CHALKER

Former Minister of Overseas Development

My favourite hymn is 'He Who Would Valiant Be Against All Disaster' because I find it both thought provoking and encouraging!

I have witnessed the great forbearance of so many people in very impoverished circumstances whom, when disaster strikes, seem to find immense inner reserves of strength. From them I have learned many lessons.

TO BE A PILGRIM

He who would valiant be
'gainst all disaster,
let him in constancy
follow the Master.
There's no discouragement
shall make him once relent,
his first avowed intent
to be a pilgrim.

Who so beset him round
with dismal stories,
so but themselves confound –
his strength the more is.
No foes shall stay his might,
though he with giants fight:
he will make good his right
to be a pilgrim.

Since, Lord, Thou dost defend
us with Thy Spirit,
we know we at the end
shall life inherit.
Then fancies flee away!
I'll fear not what men say,
I'll labour night and day
to be a pilgrim.

PERCY DEARMER (1867–1936)
AFTER JOHN BUNYON (1723–88)

From *The English Hymnal* by Permission of Oxford University Press.

BARONESS COX

'Lead us, heavenly Father, lead us, o'er this world's tempestuous sea . . .' is one of my favourites because the words remind us that our Christian faith does not offer us any protection against the challenges of life; indeed, it is a warning that there is no such thing as comfortable Christianity. However, it is a gloriously encouraging reminder that our Lord and Saviour Jesus Christ has Himself suffered the trials and tribulations of human existence and that He promised to send the Holy Spirit, the Comforter, to be with us to guide and strengthen us and to lead us in the way He has prepared for us. The hymn reminds us that the Holy Spirit brings joy and peace and, for me, this brings back memories of the radiant faith I have witnessed when I have had the privilege of being with our brothers and sisters in Christ who are suffering persecution and who worship God with irrepressible joy even in the wilderness, suffering every kind of physical deprivation.

LEAD US, HEAVENLY FATHER, LEAD US

Lead us, heavenly Father, lead us
o'er the world's tempestuous sea;
guard us, guide us, keep us, feed us –
for we have no help but Thee,
yet possessing every blessing
if our God our Father be.

Saviour, breathe forgiveness o'er us:
all our weakness Thou dost know:
Thou didst tread this earth before us,
Thou didst feel its keenest woe;
lone and dreary, faint and weary,
through the desert Thou didst go.

Spirit of our God, descending,
fill our hearts with heavenly joy,
love with every passion blending,
pleasure that can never cloy:
thus provided, pardoned, guided,
nothing can our peace destroy.

JAMES EDMESTON (1791–1867)

WENDY CRAIG

Actress

'Glad That I Live Am I' – I am in love with God's creation. Every time I go outside I am struck with awe by the beauty of the countryside. The sky, the clouds, the plants and creatures fill me with delight and wonder.

When I slip into my garden or walk across the fields, I find myself bursting with joy into this hymn. The words describe my gratitude to Him for the love and guidance He shows us.

GLAD THAT I LIVE AM I

Glad that I live am I;
That the sky is blue;
Glad for the country lanes,
And the fall of dew.

After the sun the rain,
After the rain the sun;
This is the way of life,
Till the work be done.

All that we need to do,
Be we low or high,
Is to see that we grow
Nearer the sky.

LIZETTE WOODWARD REESE (1865–1935)

JUDI DENCH

Actress

'To Be A Pilgrim' is my favourite hymn because I find it uplifting and inspiring.

TO BE A PILGRIM

Who would true valour see,
Let him come hither;
One here will constant be,
Come wind, come weather;
There's no discouragement
Shall make him once relent
His first avowed intent
To be a pilgrim.

Who so beset him round
With dismal stories,
Do but themselves confound;
His strength the more is.
No lion can him fright,
He'll with a giant fight,
But he will have a right
To be a pilgrim.

Hobgoblin nor foul fiend
Can daunt his spirit;
He knows he at the end
Shall life inherit.
Then fancies fly away!
He'll fear not what men say,
He'll labour night and day
To be a pilgrim.

PERCY DEARMER (1867_1936)
AFTER JOHN BUNYON (1628–88)

JONATHAN EDWARDS

Athlete

As a Christian, it is my earnest desire to live a life that glorifies God. The only way that I will be able to do that is if my relationship with Him is my life's priority. 'Be Thou My Vision' speaks eloquently of that kind of commitment and the all-consuming passion that I want to characterise my own walk of faith. We all need vision, a sense of purpose in life, and this hymn describes the greatest one of all.

BE THOU MY VISION

Be thou my Vision, O Lord of my heart;
Naught be all else to me, save that thou art,
Thou my best thought, by day or by night,
Waking or sleeping, thy presence my light.

Be thou my Wisdom, thou my true Word;
I ever with thee, thou with me, Lord;
Thou my great Father, I thy true son;
Thou in me dwelling, and I with thee one.

Be thou my battle-shield, sword for the fight;
Be thou my dignity, thou my delight,
Thou my soul's shelter, thou my high tower:
Raise thou me heaven-ward, O Power of my power.

Riches I heed not, nor man's empty praise,
Thou mine inheritance, now and always:
Thou and thou only, first in my heart,
High King of Heaven, my treasure thou art.

High King of Heaven, after victory won,
May I reach heaven's joys, O bright heaven's Sun!
Heart of my own heart, whatever befall,
Still be my Vision, O Ruler of all.

IRISH, C. 8TH CENTURY
TRANS. MARY BYRNE (1880–1931)
AND ELEANOR HULL (1860–1935)

A D A M   F A I T H

Television Personality

'Abide With Me' is the only hymn I learnt and the one I most favour. It has remained in my mind through childhood and to the present day.

ABIDE WITH ME

Abide with me;
fast falls the eventide;
the darkness deepens;
Lord, with me abide;
when other helpers fail,
and comforts flee,
help of the helpless, O abide with me.

Swift to its close
ebbs out life's little day;
earth's joys grown dim,
its glories pass away;
change and decay in all around I see:
O Thou who changest not,
abide with me!

I need Thy presence
every passing hour;
what but Thy grace
can foil the tempter's power?
Who like Thyself
my guide and stay can be?
Through cloud and sunshine,
O abide with me.

I fear no foe with Thee at hand to bless;
ills have no weight,
and tears no bitterness.
Where is death's sting?
where, grave, thy victory?
I triumph still, if Thou abide with me.

HENRY FRANCIS LYTE (1793–1847)

SIR RANULPH FIENNES

Explorer

My favourite hymn is 'Hills Of The North, Rejoice!' which I like because of the stirring rhythm.

HILLS OF THE NORTH, REJOICE!

Hills of the north, rejoice!
River and mountain-spring,
Hark to the advent voice;
Valley and lowland, sing!
Though absent long, your Lord is night;
He judgement brings and victory.

Isles of the southern seas,
Deep in your coral caves
Pent be each warring breeze,
Lulled be your restless waves:
He comes to reign with boundless sway,
And makes your wastes his great highway.

Lands of the east, awake!
Soon shall your sons be free;
The sleep of ages break,
And rise to liberty:
On your far hills, long and cold and grey,
Has dawned the everlasting day.

Shores of the utmost west,
Ye that have waited long,
Unvisited, unblest,
Break forth to swelling song;
High raise the note, that Jesus died,
Yet lives and reigns, the crucified.

Shout, while ye journey home!
Songs be in every mouth;
Lo, from the north we come,
From east and west and south,
City of God, the bond are free,
We come to live and reign in thee!

C E OAKLEY (1832–65)

EDDIE GEORGE

Governor of the Bank of England

Choosing 'my favourite hymn' proved to be much more difficult than I had expected – but it was a hugely enjoyable process. There really are so many magnificent hymns to choose from – magnificent tunes, deeply meaningful and moving words, a whole range of different moods and emotions, and hymns which are particularly associated with all kinds of personal experiences and events.

I finally settled on 'Now Thank We All Our God' which I can so well remember regularly singing as a boy at the top of my voice, together with the whole school – and orchestra – at our end-of-term services at Dulwich College.

The immediate reason for my choice is an overwhelming sense of relief that the brutality in Kosovo is now largely at an end. But that in itself is a very powerful reminder of our own – and my own – good fortune, and of the responsibility towards others that goes with it. And of course it is a wonderful tune.

NOW THANK WE ALL OUR GOD

Now thank we all our God,
With hearts and hands and voices,
Who wondrous things hath done,
In Whom His world rejoices;
Who, from our mother's arms,
Hath blessed us on our way
With countless gifts of love,
And still is ours today.

O may this bounteous God
Through all our life be near us,
With ever joyful hearts
And blessèd peace to cheer us;
And keep us in His grace,
And guide us when perplexed,
And free us from all ills
In this world and the next.

All praise and thanks to God
The Father now be given,
The Son, and Him Who reigns
With Them in highest heaven, –
The One eternal God,
Whom heaven and earth adore;
For thus it was, is now,
And shall be evermore.

MARTIN RINKART (1586–1649)
TRANS. CATHERINE WINKWORTH (1827-78)

JOHN GOWANS

General of the Salvation Army

When it comes to singing, Salvation Army people are incredibly cosmopolitan in their tastes. Their song book is regularly revised but the current edition of about a thousand songs contains contributions from almost every Christian denomination.

Whilst some are of a very recent date, others go back quite a long way. For instance, Bernard of Clairvaux (1091–1153) has an honoured place with his well-loved hymn, 'Jesus The Very Thought Of Thee With Sweetness Fills My Breast'. Clearly Salvationists are inveterate borrowers!

Sometimes, however, they write their own songs and my favourite is found among those written by a Salvation Army officer, Catherine Baird. The Colonel was Promoted to Glory, as we say in the Army, some years ago.

She addresses The Almighty by the name which perhaps best declares His nature, for she calls Him simply 'Love'. She writes a song of thanksgiving for the revelation God gives us of Himself in The Christ. Maybe she was inspired by Meister Eckhart's assertion that despite our best efforts we would never have

found God unless He had given Himself away in Christ.

The suggestion that we see God most clearly in Christ is a liberating one. There is great comfort to be found in the statement of Jesus: 'He who has seen me has seen The Father.' If God is like Jesus then He is a great deal kinder than we might have supposed; a great deal more understanding; a great deal more approachable.

My heart echoes to Catherine's words:
'Oh Love, invisible before,
I see Thee now, desire Thee more.'

O LOVE, REVEALED ON EARTH IN CHRIST

O love, revealed on earth in Christ,
In blindness once I sacrificed Thy gifts for dross;
I could not see,
But Jesus brings me sight of thee.
I come to thee with quiet mind,
Thyself to know, thy will to find;
In Jesus' steps my steps must be,
I follow him to follow thee.

O Love, invisible before,
I see thee now, desire thee more;
When Jesus speaks thy word is clear;
I search his face and find thee near.

O Love, for ever claim my eyes!
Thy beauty be my chosen prize;
I cast my load on timeless grace
That my free soul may run the race.

CATHERINE BAIRD (1896–1984)

ARCHBISHOP GREGORIOS

of the Greek Orthodox Church

This hymn, 'It Is The Day Of Resurrection', expresses the deeper meaning of Christianity –
 the spirit of newness,
 the spirit of renewal,
 the spirit of hope,
 the spirit of forgiveness and
 the spirit of love and eternity.

IT IS THE DAY OF RESURRECTION

It is the Day of Resurrection: let us be glorious in splendour for the Festival, and let us embrace one another. Let us speak also, O brethren, to those that hate us, and in the Resurrection, let us forgive all things, and so let us cry: Christ has risen from the dead, by death trampling upon Death, and has bestowed Life to those in the tombs.'

Ἀναστάσεως ημερα και λαμπρυνθμεν τη Πανηγυρει, και άλληλους περιπτυξωμεθα. Ειπωμεν, αδελφοι, και τοις μισουσιν ημας, συγξωρησωμεν παντα τη Ἀναστασει, και ουτω βοησωμεν Χριστος ανεοτη εκ νεκρωυ, θανατω θανατον πατησας και τοις πνηπασι ξωην χαρισαπενος.

GENERAL SIR CHARLES GUTHRIE

Chief of the Defence Staff

I went to a school which had a great tradition for choral singing and one of the hymns which I remember being sung with enormous enthusiasm in the school chapel was 'Guide Me, O Thou Great Redeemer'. When I was commissioned into the Welsh Guards I often heard and sang the hymn at regimental church services and when we were far away from home in places such as Aden, Cyprus and Libya. There were memorable occasions when I heard the hymn sung by thousands upon thousands of rugby supporters at Cardiff Arms Park; hearing the singing swirling around the stadium was exciting and certainly worth a few points on the scoreboard.

The hymn has several messages but perhaps the most important is that it reminds one of the greatness of God and the insignificance of man. The hymn shows how we need God's help for our journey through life and how he will give us strength and hope for the challenges which we will have to face before we emerge safe on the other side.

BREAD OF HEAVEN

Guide me, O thou great Redeemer,
Pilgrim through this barren land;
I am weak, but thou art mighty,
Hold me with thy powerful hand:
Bread of heaven,
Feed me till I want no more.

Open now the crystal fountain,
Whence the healing stream doth flow;
Let the fire and cloudy pillar
Lead me all my journey through:
Strong Deliverer,
Be thou still my strength and shield.

When I tread the verge of Jordan,
Bid my anxious fears subside;
Death of death, and hell's Destruction,
Land me safe on Canaan's side:
Songs of praises
I will ever give to thee.

WILLIAM WILLIAMS (1717–91)
TRANS. PETER WILLIAMS (1727–96) AND OTHERS

WILLIAM HAGUE

MP and Leader of the Opposition

'Cwm Rhondda' is my favourite hymn, and was sung at my wedding. This hymn has very special connotations for both myself and Ffion and the tune is familiar, in different versions, to both English and Welsh ears.

BREAD OF HEAVEN

Originally written in Welsh by the preacher and theologian, William Williams, this uplifting hymn was first published in 1745 and translated into English a few years later. With its wonderful Welsh tune, 'Cwm Rhondda', composed by John Hughes in 1907, the hymn has an immense universal appeal, often being sung in the open air.

SIR JOHN HARVEY-JONES

Businessman, Broadcaster and Writer

'For Those In Peril On The Sea' was the naval hymn sung at every service during my years at Dartmouth. My later years at sea confirmed the truth of the words and served continuously to remind me of the smallness of man and the mighty force of the elements.

FOR THOSE IN PERIL ON THE SEA

Eternal Father, strong to save,
whose arm hath bound
the restless wave,
who bidd'st the mighty ocean deep
its own appointed limits keep:
O hear us when we cry to Thee
for those in peril on the sea.

O Christ, whose voice the waters heard,
and hushed their raging at Thy word,
who walkedst on the foaming deep,
and calm amid the storm didst sleep:
O hear us when we cry to Thee
for those in peril on the sea.

O Holy Spirit, who didst brood
upon the waters dark and rude,
and bid their angry tumult cease,
and give, for wild confusion, peace:
O hear us when we cry to Thee
for those in peril on the sea.

O Trinity of love and power,
our brethren shield in danger's hour;
from rock and tempest, fire and foe,
protect them wheresoe'er they go:
thus evermore shall rise to Thee
glad hymns of praise from land and sea.

WILLIAM WHITING (1825–1878)

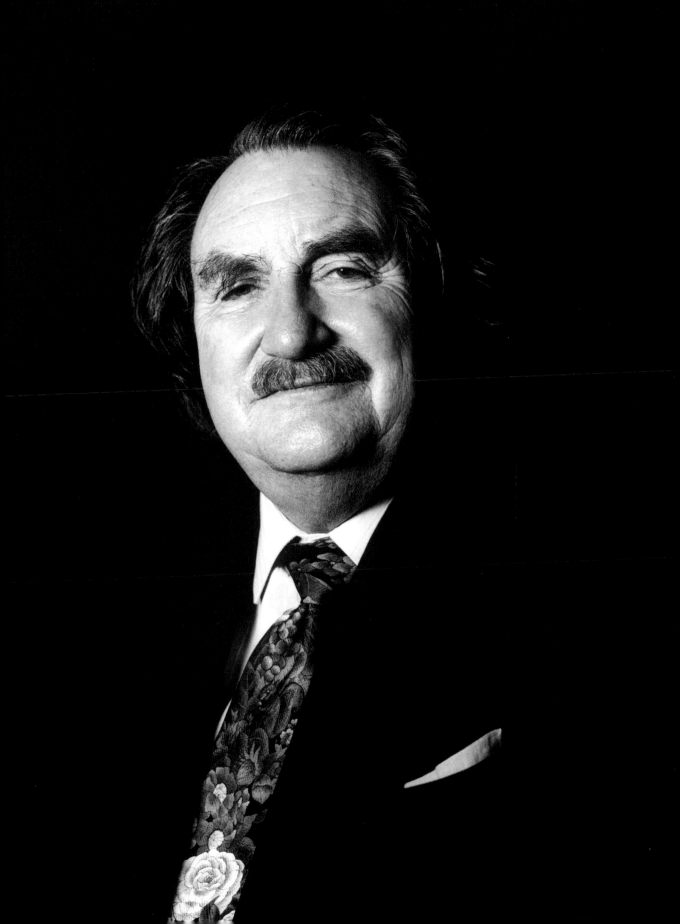

SIR EDWARD HEATH

MP and Father of the House of Commons

"My favourite hymn is 'For All The Saints Who From Their Labours Rest', by Bishop W W How in Sine Nomine with the tune by Ralph Vaughan Williams.

I regard this as one of the greatest hymn tunes of modern times and the differences between the verses of these splendid words enable the theme to be coloured differently as the hymn progresses. I must admit to being one of those who strongly support the slower tempo for the last grand verse."

FOR ALL THE SAINTS

For all the Saints
who from their labours rest,
who Thee by faith
before the world confessed,
Thy name, O Jesu, be for ever blest.
Alleluia!

Thou wast their Rock,
their fortress, and their might;
Thou, Lord, their Captain
in the well fought fight;
Thou in the darkness drear
their one true light.
Alleluia!

O may Thy soldiers,
faithful, true and bold,
fight as the Saints
who nobly fought of old,
and win, with them,
the victor's crown of gold!
Alleluia!

From earth's wide bounds,
from ocean's farthest coast,
through gates of pearl
streams in the countless host,
singing to Father, Son and Holy Ghost.
Alleluia!

WILLIAM WALSHAM HOW (1823–1897)

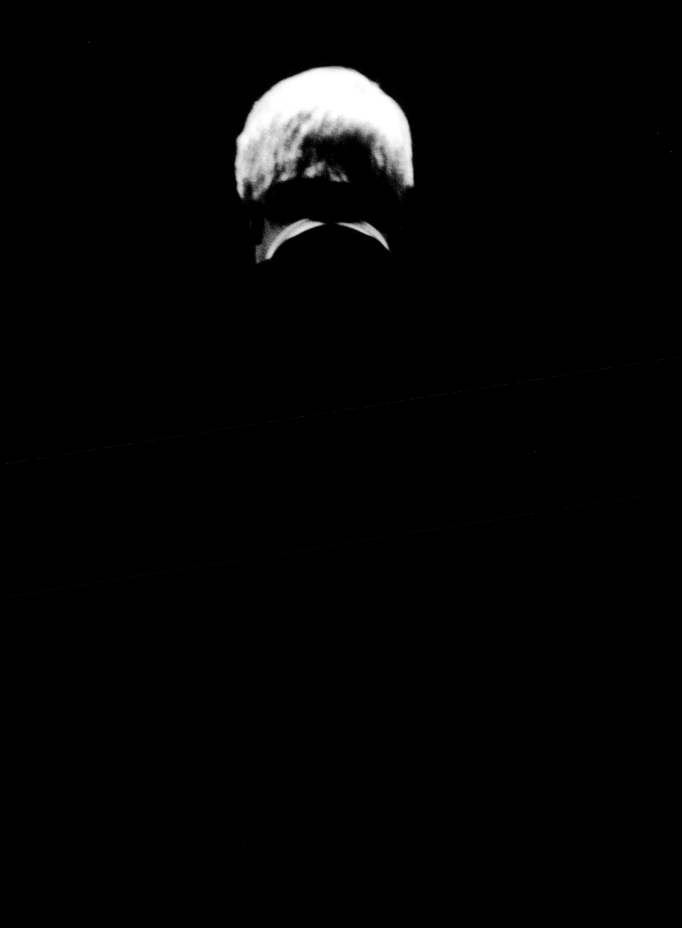

THORA HIRD

Actress

'Onward, Christian Soldiers' has followed me all the way through my life. I remember first singing it at Sunday School as a little child. It is such an enchanting tune for children.

The Salvation Army, of whom I am very fond, play it often and have twice done so especially for me. The first time was on television when they did a *This Is Your Life* programme on me. The second was at a Lady Taverners luncheon in my honour when, to my complete surprise and great delight, the band marched in playing the tune. That was very thrilling.

I do not know what I would do without God; and nor do I know who I would have been without the cross and what that stands for. But I do know that many others have been helped in the same way as I have. I thank God daily for all his love.

ONWARD, CHRISTIAN SOLDIERS

Onward, Christian soldiers,
marching as to war,
with the cross of Jesus going on before.
Christ the royal Master
leads against the foe;
forward into battle, see, His banners go!
Onward, Christian soldiers,
marching as to war,
with the cross of Jesus going on before.

At the name of Jesus
Satan's legions flee;
on then, Christian soldiers,
on to victory.
Hell's foundations quiver
at the shout of praise;
brothers, lift your voices,
loud your anthems raise.
Onward, Christian soldiers . . .

Crowns and thrones may perish,
kingdoms rise and wane,
but the Church of Jesus
constant will remain;
gates of hell can never
'gainst that Church prevail;
We have Christ's own promise,
and that cannot fail.
Onward, Christian soldiers . . .

Onward, then, ye people,
join our happy throng,
blend with ours your voices
in the triumph song;
glory, praise and honour
unto Christ the King;
This through countless ages
men and angels sing.
Onward, Christian soldiers . . .

SABINE BARING-GOULD (1834–1924)

NICOLA HORLICK

Businesswoman

'Love Divine' was sung at our wedding and at my daughter, Georgie's, funeral. Love defines those who matter most to you. Although we do not personally know those who are suffering in the Kosovan conflict, the images that we see stir feelings of emotion. Having lost a child myself, I can relate to mothers who have had their children taken away or to children who have lost their parents.

LOVE DIVINE

Love divine, all loves excelling,
joy of heaven, to earth come down:
fix in us Thy humble dwelling,
all Thy faithful mercies crown.
Jesus, Thou art all compassion,
pure, unbounded love Thou art;
visit us with Thy salvation,
enter every trembling heart.

Breathe, O breathe Thy loving Spirit
into every troubled breast;
let us all in Thee inherit,
let us find Thy promised rest.
Take away the love of sinning,
Alpha and Omega be;
end of faith, as its beginning,
set our hearts at liberty.

Come, almighty to deliver,
let us all Thy grace receive;
suddenly return, and never,
never more Thy temples leave.
Thee we would be always blessing,
serve Thee as Thy hosts above,
pray, and praise Thee without ceasing,
glory in Thy perfect love.

Finish then Thy new creation:
pure and spotless let us be;
let us see Thy great salvation,
perfectly restored in Thee:
Changed from glory into glory,
till in heaven we take our place,
till we cast our crowns before Thee,
lost in wonder, love, and praise.

CHARLES WESLEY (1707-88)

THE LATE CARDINAL HUME

Former Archbishop of Westminster

Father Michael Seed, Ecumenical Adviser to the late Cardinal Hume: 'Cardinal Hume was very ill and unable to provide more than the title, 'Lead Kindly Light' by Cardinal Newman. For me, those three simple words give us the core of the life and spirit of the late loved Cardinal Hume. In such a very gentle and humble way the Cardinal would lead us to the great light, Jesus Christ. He was a kindly man of God and loved far beyond the Christian tradition. This was because, as a Benedictine monk, he knew the gift of silence. The power of silence. He was always the monk and never, even though he was a Cardinal and thus a Prince of the Church, took himself too seriously. He was childlike in outlook and did not Jesus tell us to learn from children and never to get all puffed up as we grow older? In the 76 years the Cardinal lived on this earth he was always a loving child of God. May he rest in peace and rise in glory.'

LEAD KINDLY LIGHT

Lead kindly Light,
amid the encircling gloom,
lead Thou me on;
the night is dark,
and I am far from home;
lead Thou me on.
Keep Thou my feet; I do not ask to see
the distant scene;
one step enough for me.

I was not ever thus,
nor prayed that Thou
shouldst lead me on;
I loved to choose
and see my path; but now
lead Thou me on.
I loved the garish day,
and, spite of fears,
pride ruled my will:
remember not past years.

So long Thy power has blest me,
sure it still
will lead me on
o'er moor and fen,
o'er crag and torrent, till
the night is gone;
and with the morn
those angel faces smile
which I have loved long since,
and lost awhile.

JOHN HENRY NEWMAN (1801–90)

GLORIA HUNNIFORD

Television Personality

"I chose 'Love Divine' because it is a very special hymn in our family.

It was my mother's favourite hymn. St Mark's Church, Portadown, in Northern Ireland, played it at her funeral.

It was played at my daughter Caron's wedding.

Don, my former husband's funeral.

My wedding, last September 1998.

It means so much."

LOVE DIVINE

Love divine, all loves excelling,
joy of heaven, to earth come down:
fix in us Thy humble dwelling,
all Thy faithful mercies crown.
Jesus, Thou art all compassion,
pure, unbounded love Thou art;
visit us with Thy salvation,
enter every trembling heart.

Breathe, O breathe Thy loving Spirit
into every troubled breast;
let us all in Thee inherit,
let us find Thy promised rest.
Take away the love of sinning,
Alpha and Omega be;
end of faith, as its beginning,
set our hearts at liberty.

Come, almighty to deliver,
let us all Thy grace receive;
suddenly return, and never,
never more Thy temples leave.
Thee we would be always blessing,
serve Thee as Thy hosts above,
pray, and praise Thee without ceasing,
glory in Thy perfect love.

Finish then Thy new creation:
pure and spotless let us be;
let us see Thy great salvation,
perfectly restored in Thee:
Changed from glory into glory,
till in heaven we take our place,
till we cast our crowns before Thee,
lost in wonder, love, and praise.

CHARLES WESLEY (1707–88)

LORD IRVINE

Lord Chancellor

I was brought up in the Church of Scotland. The hymns I enjoy most are the uplifting ones. 'Onward, Christian Soldiers' is a particular favourite. I am encouraged by its confident message, whilst it teaches that nothing really worthwhile can be achieved without a struggle: the greater the effort, the more valuable the victory.

ONWARD, CHRISTIAN SOLDIERS

Onward, Christian soldiers,
marching as to war,
with the cross of Jesus going on before.
Christ the royal Master
leads against the foe;
forward into battle, see, His banners go!
Onward, Christian soldiers,
marching as to war,
with the cross of Jesus going on before.

At the name of Jesus
Satan's legions flee;
on then, Christian soldiers,
on to victory.
Hell's foundations quiver
at the shout of praise;
brothers, lift your voices,
loud your anthems raise.
Onward, Christian soldiers . . .

Like a mighty army
moves the Church of God;
brothers, we are treading
where the saints have trod;
we are not divided, all one body we,
one in hope and calling, one in charity.
Onward, Christian soldiers . . .

Onward, then, ye people,
join our happy throng,
blend with ours your voices
in the triumph song;
glory, praise and honour
unto Christ the King;
This through countless ages
men and angels sing.
Onward, Christian soldiers . . .

SABINE BARING-GOULD (1834–1924)

P D JAMES

Writer

Singing hymns was very much a part of my childhood and I have a number of favourites rather than one hymn which I love above all others. So much depends on mood, tune and the Church's liturgical season. But high among my favourites is 'For All Thy Saints Who From Their Labours Rest', a magnificent processional song of triumph usually, but not invariably, sung on All Saints' Day. The words were written by William Walsham How (1823–97) who, in 1889, became the first Bishop of the new industrial diocese of Wakefield. He was among the best loved of all Victorian clergymen, particularly for his work among the poor of the East End when he was Bishop of London.

This hymn was my mother's favourite and I never sing it without hearing echoes of her warm contralto voice. It is now usually sung to the triumphant tune by Ralph Vaughan Williams which he composed in 1906 for the hymn's first appearance in the *English Hymnal*.

FOR ALL THY SAINTS

For all Thy saints who from their labours rest,
Who Thee by faith before the world confessed,
Thy Name, O Jesus, be for ever blest. Alleluia!

Thou wast their Rock, their Fortress, and their Might;
Thou, Lord, their Captain in the well-fought fight;
Thou, in the darkness drear, their one true Light.
Alleluia!

For the Apostles' glorious company,
Who bearing forth the Cross o'er land and sea,
Shook all the mighty world, we sing to thee; Alleluia!

For the Evangelists, by whose pure word,
Like fourfold stream, the garden of the Lord,
Is fair and fruitful, by Thy name adored. Alleluia!

For Martyrs, who with rapture-kindled eye,
Saw the bright crown descending from the sky,
And, seeing, grasped it, thee we glorify. Alleluia!

O may Thy soldiers, faithful, true, and bold,
Fight as the saints who nobly fought of old,
And win, with them, the victor's crown of gold.
Alleluia!

From earth's wide bounds, from ocean's farthest coast,
Through gates of pearl streams in the countless host,
Singing to Father, Son, and Holy Ghost. Alleluia!

WILLIAM WALSHAM HOW (1823–1897)

PAUL JOHNSON

Journalist

My favourite hymn is by John Henry, Cardinal Newman, and he called it 'The Pillar of Cloud'. He wrote it on 16 June 1833 when, after his first visit to Rome, he was becalmed at sea off the coast of Sardinia, was desperately homesick, and did not know when he would reach England again. It is a poem of submission to divine providence, a cry of trust from a fiercely independent-minded and intellectually gifted man, saying he is glad to put aside all his own reasoning and doubts and qualifications, and entrust his entire being and future to the wisdom of Almighty God. It is a hymn Thomas Aquinas, the superbrain who was still humble, would have approved of, and it ought to be sung regularly by all Christian intellectuals with a tendency to grow too big for their boots.

LEAD KINDLY LIGHT

Lead kindly Light,
amid the encircling gloom,
lead Thou me on;
the night is dark,
and I am far from home;
lead Thou me on.
Keep Thou my feet; I do not ask to see
the distant scene;
one step enough for me.

I was not ever thus,
nor prayed that Thou
shouldst lead me on;
I loved to choose
and see my path; but now
lead Thou me on.
I loved the garish day,
and, spite of fears,
pride ruled my will:
remember not past years.

So long Thy power has blest me,
sure it still
will lead me on
o'er moor and fen,
o'er crag and torrent, till
the night is gone;
and with the morn
those angel faces smile
which I have loved long since,
and lost awhile.

JOHN HENRY NEWMAN (1801–90)

FELICITY KENDAL

Actress

"To watch my small son, head in hand, study his scripture is my blessing. Perhaps, in this younger generation, with learning we can find peace and understanding between the peoples of the world, between people of different beliefs."

AGADAH

On the shores of Lake Kinneret
there is a most glorious place,
a garden of God is planted there,
in which no tree moves.

Who dwells there? Only a boy
like a bird in the silent forest!
There he learns the Torah
from the mouth of Elijah.

Hush! . . . Not a wave breaks.
Every bird that flies
stands and listens –
absorbing God's Torah

R T   K E N D A L L

Minister of Westminster Chapel

As a pastor and theologian, Charles Wesley's hymn 'And Can It Be' combines every ingredient one would want in a hymn. The majesty and glory of God are set against one's feeling of awe and unworthiness. It shows what conversion is like, how we know we are saved and that there's a hope of going to Heaven one day. It is the closest you get to infallibility in hymnody!

AND CAN IT BE

And can it be that I should gain
an interest in the Saviour's blood?
Died He for me, who caused His pain?
For me, who Him to death pursued?
Amazing love! how can it be
that Thou, my God,
shouldst die for me!

'Tis mystery all! The Immortal dies:
who can explore His strange design?
In vain the first-born seraph tries
to sound the depths of love divine.
'Tis mercy all! let earth adore,
let angel minds inquire no more.

He left His Father's throne above –
so free, so infinite His grace –
emptied Himself of all but love,
and bled for Adam's helpless race.
'Tis mercy all, immense and free;
for, O my God, it found out me!

Long my imprisoned spirit lay
fast bound in sin and nature's night;
Thine eye diffused a quickening ray –
I woke, the dungeon flamed with light;
my chains fell off, my heart was free.
I rose, went forth, and followed Thee.

No condemnation now I dread;
Jesus, and all in Him, is mine!
Alive in Him, my living Head,
and clothed in righteousness divine,
bold I approached the eternal throne,
and claim the crown,
through Christ, my own.

CHARLES WELSEY (1707–88)

GRAHAM KENDRICK

Hymnist

How can a cross be wondrous? Yet to me, the hymn 'When I Survey The Wondrous Cross' is all about wonder – wonder at the seemingly mad extremes of divine love that chooses a crucifixion to atone for evil and conquer death, surely the same wonder that inspired its author nearly three centuries ago. The wonder of it, of course, depends entirely upon the identity of the victim, for if it was not the 'Prince of Glory' engaged in an extraordinary and deliberate act of redemption, then it must be something quite horrible; a two-thousand-year-running advertisement of evil triumphing over goodness and love.

As a songwriter who has attempted several hymns, I am in awe of the power of these deceptively simple stanzas which, when sung, feel so substantial, even epic, in their proportions.

As a sinner, it puts me in my place, but the place turns out to be the one place where I am offered the gift of redemption . . . more wonder!

WHEN I SURVEY THE WONDROUS CROSS

When I survey the wondrous cross,
on which the Prince of Glory died,
my richest gain I count but loss,
and pour contempt on all my pride.

Forbid it, Lord, that I should boast
save in the death of Christ my God;
all the vain things that charm me most,
I sacrifice them to His blood.

See from His head, His hands, His feet,
sorrow and love flow mingled down;
did e'er such love and sorrow meet,
or thorns compose so rich a crown?

Were the whole realm of nature mine,
that were a present far too small;
love so amazing, so divine,
demands my soul, my life, my all.

ISAAC WATTS (1674–1748)

HRH PRINCE MICHAEL OF KENT

'For All The Saints Who From Their Labours Rest' is a powerful hymn with splendid, inspiring words and a thumping good hymn tune to sing it to.

As a child our doctor and his family were called Saint and one Sunday they all arrived late for church and had to progress to their seats just as the first line of this hymn was being sung. Dr Saint told me this story himself and I have always felt for him and what a humiliating moment it must have been!

FOR ALL THE SAINTS

For all the Saints
who from their labours rest,
who Thee by faith
before the world confessed,
Thy name, O Jesu, be for ever blest.
Alleluia!

Thou wast their Rock,
their fortress, and their might;
Thou, Lord, their Captain
in the well fought fight;
Thou in the darkness drear
their one true light.
Alleluia!

O may Thy soldiers,
faithful, true and bold,
fight as the Saints
who nobly fought of old,
and win, with them,
the victor's crown of gold!
Alleluia!

O blest communion, fellowship divine!
We feebly struggle, they in glory shine;
yet all are one in Thee,
for all are Thine.
Alleluia!

From earth's wide bounds,
from ocean's farthest coast,
through gates of pearl
streams in the countless host,
singing to Father, Son and Holy Ghost.
Alleluia!

WILLIAM WALSHAM HOW (1823–1897)

ERIC KNOWLES

Antiques Expert and Broadcaster

'I Vow To Thee My Country', from the *Planet Suite* by Gustav Holst is a very evocative hymn – what I would call 'picture music'. It is a lovely blending of poetry with music.

I VOW TO THEE MY COUNTRY

I vow to thee my country,
all earthly things above,
entire and whole and perfect,
the service of my love:
the love that asks no questions,
the love that stands the test,
that lays upon the altar
the dearest and the best;
the love that never falters,
the love that pays the price,
the love that makes undaunted
the final sacrifice.

And there's another country,
I've heard of long ago,
most dear to them that love her,
most great to them that know;
we may not count her armies,
we may not see her King;
her fortress is a faithful heart,
her pride is suffering;
and soul by soul and silently
her shining bounds increase,
and her ways are ways of gentleness
and all her paths are peace.

CECIL SPRING-RICE (1859–1918)

FRANCES LAWRENCE

Teacher, Founder of The Philip Lawrence Award

As a child I responded to 'To Be A Pilgrim' as if it were a legend or a fable. The cast of characters – hobgoblins and lions, foul fiends and giants – conjured up a dark and unfamiliar universe, far removed from the safety of the church in which we sang about them.

It was only years later that the murder of my husband brought those fairy-tale images sharply into focus and grounded them in reality.

Each one of us, they seem to say, has a pilgrimage to make. Along the way there are many dangers to confront and many dragons to slay: it will be difficult but we must not listen to sceptics who proclaim that there is nothing to be done. Instead we must stretch across the streets of violence, fighting not with our fists but with the integrity of the human spirit.

If we have the courage to make this pilgrimage an integral part of our daily lives, perhaps we shall overcome the vanity of the material world and discover a more sacred destination.

TO BE A PILGRIM

Who would true valour see,
Let him come hither;
One here will constant be,
Come wind, come weather;
There's no discouragement
Shall make him once relent
His first avowed intent
To be a pilgrim.

Who so beset him round
With dismal stories,
Do but themselves confound;
His strength the more is.
No lion can him fright,
He'll with a giant fight,
But he will have a right
To be a pilgrim.

Hobgoblin nor foul fiend
Can daunt his spirit;
He knows he at the end
Shall life inherit.
Then fancies fly away!
He'll fear not what men say,
He'll labour night and day
To be a pilgrim.

PERCY DEARMER (1867–1936)
AFTER JOHN BUNYAN (1628–88)

From *The English Hymnal* by permission of Oxford University Press.

MAUREEN LIPMAN

Actress and Writer

'Lord Dismiss Us With Thy Blessing' would be played on the last day of term at my grammar school and it would always make me weep.

Somehow the last days of term had a freeform, jazzy quality, particularly the end of the summer term, when rigid class structures were fractured, plays were performed and rules bent.

Friendships seemed both precious and eternal and yet, from the words of this hymn, I knew that was not the case.

LORD DISMISS US WITH THY BLESSING

Lord dismiss us with Thy blessing,
Fill our hearts with joy and peace;
Let us each, Thy love possessing,
Triumph in redeeming grace:
Oh, refresh us!
Travelling through this wilderness.

Thanks we give, and adoration,
For the gospel's joyful sound;
May the fruits of Thy salvation
In our hearts and lives abound;
May Thy presence
With us, evermore, be found.

So, whene'er the signal's given
Us from earth to call away;
Borne on angels' wings to heaven
Glad the summons to obey,
May we ever
Reign with Thee in endless day.

ATTRIBUTED TO JOHN FAWCETT, 1773 (altd)

JOANNA LUMLEY

Actress

'Immortal, invisible, God only wise' – absolutely stunning and I love the words more than I can say. Any hymn which starts with the word 'immortal' gets my vote.

IMMORTAL, INVISIBLE

Immortal, invisible, God only wise,
in light inaccessible hid from our eyes,
most blessed, most glorious,
the Ancient of Days,
almighty, victorious,
Thy great name we praise.

Unresting, unhasting,
and silent as light,
nor wanting, nor wasting,
Thou rulest in might;
Thy justice like mountains
high soaring above
Thy clouds, which are fountains
of goodness and love.

To all, life Thou givest,
to both great and small;
in all life Thou livest, the true life of all;
we blossom and flourish
as leaves on the tree,
and wither and perish,
but nought changeth Thee.

Immortal, invisible, God only wise,
in light inaccessible hid from our eyes,
most blessed, most glorious,
the Ancient of Days,
almighty, victorious,
Thy great name we praise.

W CHALMERS-SMITH (1824–1908)

TREVOR McDONALD

Broadcaster

Both the music and words of 'Abide With Me' are wonderful. It's the only hymn I know that has true universality and is international. The fact is that it's sung at ceremonies around the world and also sung at football matches as well as churches.

ABIDE WITH ME

Abide with me;
fast falls the eventide;
the darkness deepens;
Lord, with me abide;
when other helpers fail,
and comforts flee,
help of the helpless, O abide with me.

Swift to its close
ebbs out life's little day;
earth's joys grown dim,
its glories pass away;
change and decay in all around I see:
O Thou who changest not,
abide with me!

I need Thy presence
every passing hour;
what but Thy grace
can foil the tempter's power?
Who like Thyself
my guide and stay can be?
Through cloud and sunshine,
O abide with me.

I fear no foe with Thee at hand to bless;
ills have no weight,
and tears no bitterness.
Where is death's sting?
where, grave, thy victory?
I triumph still, if Thou abide with me.

HENRY FRANCIS LYTE (1793–1874)

SUE MacGREGOR

Broadcaster

'Come Down, O Love Divine' is often used at Church of England weddings, and indeed ordinary services, but that's not my main reason for choosing it, lapsed Anglican that I am.

I like it because it brings back very strongly each time I hear it the pleasures of singing in the school choir, many decades ago. I went to a Church of England girls' school in Cape Town, South Africa which, although it didn't give us a very good education academically, did enthuse us – or those of us who had half an ear for music – with a delight in choral singing. We had a very good music teacher called Miss Sweet who must have been very young then, because she's only just retired. But she did a fine job with what must have been a rather unpromising bunch of schoolgirls, and made singing in church a pleasurable experience.

COME DOWN, O LOVE DIVINE

Come down, O love divine,
seek Thou this soul of mine
and visit it
with Thine own ardour glowing;
O Comforter, draw near,
within my heart appear,
and kindle it,
Thy holy flame bestowing.

O let it freely burn,
till earthly passions turn
to dust and ashes, in its heat consuming;
and let Thy glorious light
shine ever on my sight,
and clothe me round,
the while my path illuming.

Let holy charity
mine outward vesture be,
and lowliness become
mine inner clothing;
true lowliness of heart,
which takes the humbler part,
and o'er its own shortcomings
weeps with loathing.

And so the yearning strong,
with which the soul will long,
shall far outpass
the power of human telling;
for none can guess its grace,
till he become the place
wherein the Holy Spirit
makes His dwelling.

BIANCO da SIENA (d. 1434)
TRANS. R F LITTLEDALE (1833–90)

LORD MACKAY

Former Lord Chancellor

Psalm Twenty-three was among the first pieces I committed to memory as a child and its calm has strongly attracted me ever since. It is in common use for occasions of high emotion such as weddings and funerals and there is material in it for many different circumstances.

The idea of our Lord being our Shepherd is a rich source of comfort and strength. With the background of Israel in David's day it gives us a sense of provision and protection in this life. It looks to the highs and lows of our ordinary activity with our need for restoration of soul and a quiet stilling time by the water. It takes us forward to death and the wonderful presence of the Lord with his people in that dark valley and beyond that to being with the Lord in His house for ever. In the meantime, there is the comfort of provision in inhospitable circumstances and in the face of enemies.

David was described as the sweet psalmist of Israel, and this is surely one of the best known and best loved of his psalms.

Whatever our circumstances there is here a message to sustain us that does not lose its force and immediacy with the passing years.

THE LORD'S MY SHEPHERD

The Lord's my Shepherd,
I'll not want;
He makes me down to lie
in pastures green; He leadeth me
the quiet waters by.

My soul He doth restore again,
and me to walk doth make
within the paths of righteousness,
e'en for His own name's sake.

Yea, thou I walk through death's dark vale,
yet will I fear none ill,
For Thou art with me, and Thy rod,
and staff me comfort still.

My table Thou has furnished
in presence of my foes;
my head Thou dost with oil anoint,
and my cup overflows.

Goodness and mercy all my life
shall surely follow me;
and in God's house for evermore
my dwelling-place shall be.

SCOTTISH PSALTER, 1650
BASED ON PSALM 23

J O H N   M A J O R

MP and Former Prime Minister

My favourite hymn is 'Abide With Me'.
The hymn is based on a story about a
cleric who was dying as he walked
around the Norfolk coast, and I find this
immensely moving.

ABIDE WITH ME

Abide with me;
fast falls the eventide;
the darkness deepens;
Lord, with me abide;
when other helpers fail,
and comforts flee,
help of the helpless, O abide with me.

Swift to its close
ebbs out life's little day;
earth's joys grown dim,
its glories pass away;
change and decay in all around I see:
O Thou who changest not,
abide with me!

I need Thy presence
every passing hour;
what but Thy grace
can foil the tempter's power?
Who like Thyself
my guide and stay can be?
Through cloud and sunshine,
O abide with me.

Hold Thou Thy cross
before my closing eyes,
shine through the gloom,
and point me to the skies;
heaven's morning breaks,
and earth's vain shadows flee:
in life, in death, O Lord, abide with me!

HENRY FRANCIS LYTE (1793–1847)

SALLY MAGNUSSON

Television Presenter

"'The Lord Bless Thee And Keep Thee' is a blessing sung often in Church of Scotland services, particularly after a baby has been baptised, and I have always found it exquisitely moving. It is sung slowly, its melody as simple as the words themselves. There can be no more profound or more lovely blessing than this."

THE LORD BLESS THEE AND KEEP THEE

The Lord bless thee and keep thee.
The Lord make his face to shine upon thee
And be gracious unto thee.
The Lord lift up His countenance upon thee
And give thee peace.

NUMBERS 6 VV 24–26 (AV)

LAURENCE MARKS

Scriptwriter

When I was ten years old I was chosen as the principal soloist at the junior school's Christmas festival. This event always took place in the local church, and on this December day I was to give a soprano rendition of 'Once In Royal David's City'.

As I reached the words 'Mary was that mother mild, Jesus Christ . . .' I saw my mother marching furiously along the aisle. Upon the words 'Jesus Christ' she grabbed me by my surplice and frog-marched me out of the church, and there in the street gave me perhaps the greatest telling-off I had ever received. I have not to this day established just how she knew I was singing in this church! I think she was a witch and knew everything . . .

You see I was Jewish. And nice Jewish boys are not supposed to sing 'Once In Royal David's City' in the local Anglican church, Christmas or no Christmas!

When I started at my grammar school my mother gave strict instructions to the Headmaster that I was not under any circumstances to go to morning service, recite the Lord's Prayer, sing any hymns, or mention the name of Jesus Christ. I never did. The wrath of my mother's fury was too frightful to behold.

I therefore was not brought up in a house or environment where hymns were sung or even listened to, rather I started hearing them much later in life, long after both my parents had died. And whilst it might not be a hymn, as such, I always think of churches and congregations, and happiness, passion and joy, when I hear Johann Sebastian Bach's *Zion hort die Wachter singen* (Zion hears the watchman's voices). This piece of music that comes from Bach's *Cantata No. 10*, deals with the parable of the wise and foolish virgins, of whom I knew many in my adolescence. And with none of them could I reverse their situation.

Why this piece of music moves me as it does I really do not know, but on those days when I am feeling as if a dark cloud hangs over me, for whatever may be the reason, I play this wonderful composition and as of the moment it strikes up the first note, the sun begins to shine for me.

I think of all the pieces of religious music that I know, it would be *Zion hort die Wachter singen* that I would like

played at my funeral, for I believe it would guide me on a safe passage to Heaven. I just hope that my mother, already resident up there, doesn't hear me listening to it.
Here endeth.

ZION HEARS THE WATCHMEN CALLING

Zion hears the watchmen calling
The Faithful hark with joy enthralling.
They rise and haste to greet their Lord.
See, he comes, the Lord victorious,
Almighty noble, true and glorious,
In Heaven supreme, on earth adored.
Come now, Thou Holy One,
The Lord Jehovah's Son!
Alleluja!
We follow all the joyful call
To join Him in the Banquet Hall!

BACH'S CANTATA NO. 10
TRANS. LAURENCE MARKS

PIERS MORGAN

Editor of the *Daily Mirror*

For my wedding it was 'Jerusalem' – the most uplifting, tub-thumping, patriotic and inspirational hymn of all.

For my funeral I'd like 'Onward, Christian Soldiers' – may as well go out as if you mean it.

For a moment never to forget, 50,000 Welshmen singing 'Bread Of Heaven' at Cardiff Arms Park.

BREAD OF HEAVEN

Guide me, O thou great Redeemer,
Pilgrim through this barren land;
I am weak, but thou art mighty,
Hold me with thy powerful hand:
Bread of heaven,
Feed me till I want no more.

Open now the crystal fountain,
Whence the healing stream doth flow;
Let the fire and cloudy pillar
Lead me all my journey through:
Strong Deliverer,
Be thou still my strength and shield.

When I tread the verge of Jordan,
Bid my anxious fears subside;
Death of death, and hell's Destruction,
Land me safe on Canaan's side:
Songs of praises
I will ever give to thee.

WILLIAM WILLIAMS (1717–91)
TRANS. PETER WILLIAMS (1727–96) AND OTHERS

SIR JOHN MORTIMER

Author

Having been born without a religious sense, I judge hymns as more or less successful light verse. I think Reginald Heber (Bishop of Calcutta) did rather well with 'Greenland's Icy Mountain' which contains the line: 'The heathen, in his blindness, bows down to wood and stone.' Kipling rewrote this:

The 'eathen in his blindness bows
    down to wood an' stone,
'E don't obey no orders unless they is
    'is own.

I have always felt a good deal of sympathy for the heathen.

FROM GREENLAND'S ICY MOUNTAINS

From Greenland's icy mountains,
From India's coral strand,
Where Africa's sunny fountains
Roll down their golden sand;
From many an ancient river,
From many a palmy plain,
They call us to deliver
Their land from error's chain.

What though the spicy breezes
Blow soft o'er Ceylon's isle;
Though every prospect pleases,
And only man is vile;
In vain with lavish kindness
The gifts of God are strown;
The heathen, in his blindness,
Bows down to wood and stone!

Can we, whose souls are lighted
With wisdom from on high,
Can we, to men benighted
The lamp of life deny?
Salvation! yea, salvation!
The joyful sound proclaim,
Till each remotest nation
Has learned Messiah's name.

Waft, waft, ye winds, His story;
And you, ye waters roll,
Till, like a sea of glory,
It spreads from pole to pole!

Till o'er our ransomed nature,
The Lamb for sinner's slain,
Redeemer, King, Creator,
In bliss returns to reign!

REGINALD HEBER (1783–1826)

STIRLING MOSS

Motor-racing Legend

'Praise, My Soul, The King Of Heaven' would come quite high up on my list. For me, a hymn should have words that I can comfortably understand, give the spirit a lift, be nice and easy to sing (for those of limited vocal talents, such as myself) and have a jolly good tune. Very importantly, the melody has to be good enough to ensure that no more modern composer is going to have a go at changing it. There is nothing I hate more than noting on a Service Sheet a hymn I know and enjoy, only to find I can't sing along at all because the tune has been changed beyond all recognition!

PRAISE, MY SOUL, THE KING OF HEAVEN

Praise my soul,
the King of heaven;
to His feet thy tribute bring;
ransomed, healed, restored, forgiven,
who like thee His praise should sing?
Praise Him! Praise Him!
Praise Him! Praise Him!
Praise the everlasting King.

Praise Him for His grace and favour
to our fathers, in distress;
praise Him still the same for ever,
slow to chide, and swift to bless.
Praise Him! Praise Him!
Praise Him! Praise Him!
Glorious in His faithfulness.

Father-like He tends and spares us;
well our feeble frame He knows;
in His hands He gently bears us,
rescues us from all our foes.
Praise Him! Praise Him!
Praise Him! Praise Him!
Widely as His mercy flows.

Angels help us to adore Him;
ye behold Him face to face;
sun and moon, bow down before Him;
dwellers all in time and space.
Praise Him! Praise Him!
Praise Him! Praise Him!
Praise with us the God of grace.

HENRY FRANCIS LYTE (1793–1847)
BASED ON PSALM 103

JULIA NEUBERGER

Rabbi

My favourite hymn is the Twenty-third Psalm, because it is a well-known psalm that most people know bits of – the Lord's my shepherd I'll not want – but it does not get reduced to being banal, and is seriously comforting when people are grieving, or when they are troubled. And both the traditional Hebrew melody and Crimond are moving and comforting tunes.

THE LORD'S MY SHEPHERD

The Lord's my Shepherd,
I'll not want;
He makes me down to lie
in pastures green; He leadeth me
the quiet waters by.

My soul He doth restore again,
and me to walk doth make
within the paths of righteousness,
e'en for His own name's sake.

Yea, thou I walk
through death's dark vale,
yet will I fear none ill,
for Thou art with me, and Thy rod
and staff me comfort still.

My table Thou has furnished
in presence of my foes;
my head Thou dost with oil anoint,
and my cup overflows.

Goodness and mercy all my life
shall surely follow me;
and in God's house for evermore
my dwelling-place shall be.

SCOTTISH PSALTER, 1650
BASED ON PSALM 23

L O R D   O W E N

Diplomat

The hymn – 'The Day You Gave Us' –
has the merit of a simple rhythm which
allows it to be sung without musical
accompaniment and even by oneself
alone with nature. It speaks of the voice
of prayer being never silent and of a
church worldwide unsleeping across
each continent and island. This reminds
me of the living Christian message and
example twenty-four hours a day, seven
days a week, for century after century. I
believe in ecumenicism and find peace in
any place of worship whatever its
denomination anywhere in the world.
Kosovo needs, as does most of the
former Yugoslavia, to develop
religious tolerance and respect for all
faiths.

THE DAY YOU GAVE US

The day you gave us, Lord, is ended,
the sun is sinking in the west;
to you our morning hymns ascended,
your praise shall sanctify our rest.

We thank you that your church, unsleeping
while earth rolls onward into light,
through all the world her watch is keeping
and rest not now by day or night.

As to each continent and island
the dawn proclaims another day,
the voice of prayer is never silent,
nor dies the sound of praise away.

The sun that bids us rest is waking
your church beneath the western sky;
fresh voices hour by hour are making
your mighty deeds resound on high.

So be it, Lord: your throne shall never,
like earth's proud empires, pass away;
your kingdom stands, and grows for ever,
until there dawns that glorious day.

JOHN ELLERTON (1826–93)

ELAINE PAIGE

Actress and Singer

"I used to sing 'To Be A Pilgrim' at school and it was my favourite. For this particular book, I think it is most appropriate."

TO BE A PILGRIM

He who would valiant be
'gainst all disaster,
let him in constancy
follow the Master.
There's no discouragement
shall make him once relent,
his first avowed intent
to be a pilgrim.

Who so beset him round
with dismal stories,
so but themselves confound –
his strength the more is.
No foes shall stay his might,
though he with giants fight:
he will make good his right
to be a pilgrim.

Since, Lord, Thou dost defend
us with Thy Spirit,
we know we at the end
shall life inherit.
Then fancies flee away!
I'll fear not what men say,
I'll labour night and day
to be a pilgrim.

PERCY DEARMER (1867–1936)
AFTER JOHN BUNYAN (1628–88)

From *The English Hymnal* by permission of Oxford University Press.

CAROLINE PARR

Brtish Red Cross Volunteer

"I have chosen 'Dear Lord and Father of Mankind' because apart from the tune, which I adore, the words bring out the need in this hectic world to find an oasis of peace and calm to which one can retreat and retrench. It was the opening hymn at our wedding in Scotland at the end of May, and has great significance for us both."

DEAR LORD AND FATHER OF MANKIND

Dear Lord and Father of mankind,
Forgive our foolish ways!
Re-clothe us in our rightful mind,
In purer lives thy service find,
In deeper reverence praise.

In simple trust like theirs who heard,
Beside the Syrian sea,
The gracious calling of the Lord,
Let us, like them, without a word
Rise and follow thee.

Drop thy still dews of quietness,
Till all our strivings cease;
Take from our souls the strain and stress,
And let our ordered lives confess
The beauty of thy peace.

Breathe through the beats of our desire
Thy coolness and thy balm;
Let sense be dumb, let flesh retire;
Speak through the earthquake, wind, and fire,
O still small voice of calm!

J G WHITTIAR (1807–92)

MICHAEL PORTILLO

Politician

As a child, I didn't much enjoy going to mass.

True, the music usually penetrated my reverie – partly perhaps because the choir was a bit shrill, poor things. But at communion time I was uplifted by a deeply affecting tune, a song that caught up the emotions even of a bored child. A baritone voice, more histrionic than beautiful, filled Edgware Catholic Church with the sound of Cesar Franck's 'Panis Angelicus'.

Church was a family outing, except that my mother made her separate way to the Anglican church. My father took my three older brothers and me: we almost filled a pew on our own. But more exciting still was when my father joined in singing 'Panis Angelicus', a little hesitant about keeping the tune, but fluently intoning the Latin in his rich Spanish accent.

Now 'Panis Angelicus' regularly features in Classic FM's top ten. But for me, it remains special and evocative.

PANIS ANGELICUS

Panis angelicus, fit panis hominum
Dat panis caelicus, figuris terminum.
Manducat Dominum,
Pauper, pauper, servus et humilis,
Pauper, pauper, servus et humilis.

Panis angelicus, fit panis hominum,
Dat panis caelicus figuris terminum.
O res mirabilis, manducat Dominum,
Pauper, pauper, servis et humilis.

Thus Angel's Bread is made
the Bread of man today;
the Living Bread from heaven
with figures dost away;
O wondrous gift indeed!
the poor and lowly may
upon their Lord and Master feed.
Thee, therefore, we implore,
O Godhead, One in Three,
so may Thou visit us
as we worship Thee;
and lead us on Thy way;
the light wherein Thou dwellest aye.

LISA POTTS

Heroine

A lady from my church sent me 'I Know Who Holds The Future' in a letter when I was in hospital after the awful machete attack on 8 July 1996. As I read the words of the chorus, I realised that everything in my life is planned by God and as the words say: 'As I face tomorrow, With its problems large and small, I'll trust the God of miracles, Give to him my all.'

This hymn made me realise that no matter what, God is always there through the happy times and the sad times.

I KNOW WHO HOLDS THE FUTURE

I do not know what lies ahead,
The way I cannot see;
Yet one stands near to be my guide,
He'll show the way to me.
I know who holds the future,
And He'll guide me with His hand,
With God things don't just happen,
Ev'rything by Him is planned;
So as I face tomorrow
With its problems large and small,
I'll trust the God of miracles,
Give to Him my all.

I do not know how many days,
Of life are mine to spend;
But one who knows and cares for me
Will keep me to the end:
I know who holds the future . . .

I do not know the course ahead,
What joys and griefs are there;
But one is near who fully knows,
I'll trust His loving care:
I know who holds the future . . .

ALFRED SMITH AND EUGENE CLARKE

BARONESS PATRICIA RAWLINGS

Politician and Chairman of King's College

I have few regrets in my life, but one that has remained with me for ever is not being able to play the piano or any musical instrument or, worse still, being unable to sing in tune. I failed every term my audition to join the school choir. In 1970, I tried once again to learn the piano with a marvellous teacher called Peter Skellern. I had reached Grade 5 at school, but soon realised it was a losing battle. As much as I loved music, I had zero talent.

Some of the most sublime music is church music, but like choosing desert island discs, to choose one hymn is practically impossible. My favourite, I suppose, therefore, is 'Immortal, Invisible'.

I used to play this hymn once a term on the piano for around eight years at school for assembly with 'Heart Of Oak' as the march. As a result, it is the only tune that I can still play!

IMMORTAL, INVISIBLE

Immortal, invisible, God only wise,
in light inaccessible hid from our eyes,
most blessed, most glorious,
the Ancient of Days,
almighty, victorious,
Thy great name we praise.

Unresting, unhasting,
and silent as light,
nor wanting, nor wasting,
Thou rulest in might;
Thy justice like mountains
high soaring above
Thy clouds, which are fountains
of goodness and love.

To all, life Thou givest,
to both great and small;
in all life Thou livest, the true life of all;
we blossom and flourish
as leaves on the tree,
and wither and perish,
but nought changeth Thee.

Immortal, invisible, God only wise,
in light inaccessible hid from our eyes,
most blessed, most glorious,
the Ancient of Days,
almighty, victorious,
Thy great name we praise.

W CHALMERS-SMITH (1824–1908)

PAM RHODES

Presenter of *Songs of Praise*

This is a very simple children's hymn, sung every year at our local junior school. I can't think of a better hope for the new millennium than the first two lines of this song. 'Let there be peace on earth – and let it begin with me.' We're inclined to think that other people start wars, hold grudges or are indifferent and dogmatic. I believe that peace can only become a reality if each of us plays our part – peace in our homes, peace in our lives, peace in our hearts.

LET THERE BE PEACE ON EARTH

Let there be peace on earth
And let it begin with me;
Let there be peace on earth,
The peace that was meant to be.

With God as our Father,
Brothers all are we.
Let me walk with my brother
In perfect harmony.

Let peace begin with me
Let this be the moment now.
With every step I take,
Let this be my solemn vow:

To take each moment
And live each moment
In peace eternally.

Let there be peace on earth
And let it begin with me.
Let it begin with me.

SY MILLER AND JILL JACKSON

SIR TIM RICE

Songwriter

‘Onward, Christian Soldiers’ was my favourite hymn at school and I always looked forward to hymn 105 being called out. To this day I love it because it is wonderfully stirring and arousing.

ONWARD, CHRISTIAN SOLDIERS

Onward, Christian soldiers,
marching as to war,
with the cross of Jesus going on before.
Christ the royal Master
leads against the foe;
forward into battle, see, His banners go!
Onward, Christian soldiers,
marching as to war,
with the cross of Jesus going on before.

At the name of Jesus
Satan's legions flee;
on then, Christian soldiers,
on to victory.
Hell's foundations quiver
at the shout of praise;
brothers, lift your voices,
loud your anthems raise.
Onward, Christian soldiers . . .

Crowns and thrones may perish,
kingdoms rise and wane,
but the Church of Jesus
constant will remain;
gates of hell can never
’gainst that Church prevail;
We have Christ's own promise,
and that cannot fail.
Onward, Christian soldiers . . .

Onward, then, ye people,
join our happy throng,
blend with ours your voices
in the triumph song;
glory, praise and honour
unto Christ the King;
This through countless ages
men and angels sing.
Onward, Christian soldiers . . .

SABINE BARING-GOULD (1834–1924)

SIR CLIFF RICHARD

Singer

"My favourite hymn is 'When I Survey The Wondrous Cross' because, in the simplest of words, it sums up the heart of the Christian gospel."

WHEN I SURVEY THE WONDROUS CROSS

When I survey the wondrous cross
on which the Prince of glory died,
my richest gain I count but loss,
and pour contempt on all my pride.

Forbid it, Lord, that I should boast,
save in the death of Christ my God:
all the vain things that charm me most,
I sacrifice them to His blood.

See from His head, His hands, His feet,
sorrow and love flow mingled down:
did e'er such love and sorrow meet,
or thorns compose so rich a crown?

Were the whole realm of nature mine,
that were an offering far too small,
love so amazing, so divine,
demands my soul, my life, my all.

ISAAC WATTS (1674–1748)

ANGELA RIPPON

Broadcaster

'Morning Has Broken' is a wonderful, cheerful and optimistic hymn, full of good things that come our way.

MORNING HAS BROKEN

Morning has broken
like the first morning;
blackbird has spoken
like the first bird.
Praise for the singing!
Praise for the morning!
Praise for them, springing
fresh from the Word!

Sweet the rain's new fall
sunlit from heaven,
like the first dewfall
on the first grass.
Praise for the sweetness
of the wet garden,
sprung in completeness
where His feet pass.

Mine is the sunlight!
Mine is the morning
born of the one light
Eden saw play!
Praise with elation,
praise every morning,
God's re-creation
of the new day!

ELEANOR FARJEON (1881–1965)

From *The Children's Bells* published by Oxford University Press.

ANITA RODDICK

Businesswoman

I love 'O Happy Day!' because it is joyful, celebratory, uplifting and full of wonderment. Enough said!

O HAPPY DAY!

O happy day! that fixed my choice
on Thee, my Saviour and my God!
Well may this glowing heart rejoice,
and tell its raptures all abroad.
O happy day! O happy day!
when Jesus washed my sins away;
He taught me how to watch and pray,
and live rejoicing every day;
(hallelujah!)
O happy day! O happy day!
when Jesus washed my sins away.

'Tis done, the great transaction's done!
I am my Lord's and He is mine!
He drew me, and I followed on,
charmed to confess the voice divine.
O happy day . . .

Now rest, my long divided heart,
fixed on this blissful centre, rest;
nor ever from the Lord depart,
with Him of every good possessed.
O happy day . . .

PHILIP DODDRIDGE (1702–51)

LEONARD ROSOMON

Artist

"I chose 'Thy Hand, O God, Has Guided' as I had painted the vaulted ceiling in the Lambeth Palace chapel in 1987. The hymn works on two levels. Firstly, the hand of the painter being guided by God to produce the work. On the second, the ceiling itself shows the history of the Anglican Church, throughout the ages."

THY HAND, O GOD, HAS GUIDED

Thy hand, O God, has guided
thy flock, from age to age;
the wondrous tale is written,
full clear on ev'ry page;
our forebears owned thy goodness
and we their deeds record;
and both of this bear witness:
one Church, one Faith, one Lord.

Thy heralds brought glad tidings
to greatest, as to least;
they bade them rise, and hasten
to share the great King's feast;
and this was all their teaching,
in ev'ry deed and word,
to all alike proclaiming:
one Church, one Faith, one Lord.

Through many a day of darkness,
through many a scene of strife,
the faithful few fought bravely
to guard the nation's life.
Their gospel of redemption,
sin pardoned, hope restored,
was all in this enfolded:
one Church, one Faith, one Lord.

Thy mercy will not fail us,
nor leave thy work undone;
with thy right hand to help us,
the vict'ry shall be won;
and then by all creation,
thy name shall be adored.
And this shall be their anthem:
one Church, one Faith, one Lord.

EDWARD PLUMPTRE (1821–91) (altd)

JONATHAN SACKS

The Chief Rabbi

These words, among the most famous and best loved ever written, are said in many contexts in the Jewish liturgy. But for me the most moving is when they are sung as a hymn at *seudah shlishit*, the 'third meal' of the Sabbath on Saturday afternoon, as the day of rest draws to a close, the sun sets and night begins to fall.

For Jews in many countries at many times, the Sabbath was a refuge of peace in the midst of a dangerous, threatening and unpredictable world. What kept them going, regularly renewing their spirit, was the Sabbath, their oasis of rest and reflection, when they sat around the table with their family or joined the community in study and prayer and for a day they could feel they belonged to a larger and more peaceful world.

But every Sabbath ends. And as the day faded and Jews prepared to face the uncertainty of the coming week, they would sing this psalm at the afternoon meal – knowing, literally, that this was the table God had prepared for them in the presence of their enemies, and hoping that its serene promise would stay with them in the days to come.

I will never forget how, together with a group of Russian immigrants, we sang it one Sabbath afternoon in Jerusalem during the Gulf War, knowing that any minute a new SCUD missile attack might send us scurrying for safety in our sealed rooms. Somehow, the words and music worked their magic, as they always do.

As this bloodstained century draws to its close, more than ever we need its message. None of us, after the Holocaust, can take an innocent view of human nature.

THE LORD IS MY SHEPHERD

מזמור לדוד ה' רעי לא אחסר; בנאות דשא ירביצני
על מי מנוחת ינחלני נפשי ישובב ינחני במעגלי צדק
למען שמו; גם כאלך בגיא צלמות לא אירא רע כי
אתה עמדי שבטך ומשנתך המה ינחמני; תערך לפני
שלחן נגד צררי דשנת בשמן ראשי כוסי רויה; אך
טוב וחסד ירדפוני כל ימי חיי ושבתי בבית ה'
לארך ימים;

*The words to 'The Lord's My Shepherd' appear in English on page 130.

ROBERT SANGSTER

International Horse Racer and Breeder

"'There Is A Green Hill Far Away' is a great help to me and the children going through a marital crisis."

THERE IS A GREEN HILL FAR AWAY

There is a green hill far away
without a city wall,
where the dear Lord was crucified,
who died to save us all.

We may not know, we cannot tell
what pains He had to bear;
but we believe it was for us
He hung and suffered there.

He died that we might be forgiven,
He died to make us good,
that we might go at last to heaven,
saved by His precious blood.

There was no other good enough
to pay the price of sin;
He only could unlock the gate
of heaven, and let us in.

Oh, dearly, dearly has He loved,
and we must love Him too;
and trust in His redeeming blood,
and try His works to do.

PERCY DEARMER (1867–1936)
AFTER JOHN BUNYAN (1628–88)

PETER de SAVARY

Entrepreneur

My favourite hymn is 'Onward, Christian Soldiers' because this hymn reflects my personality.

ONWARD, CHRISTIAN SOLDIERS

In the words of its author, Sabine Baring-Gould, this rousing hymn was 'written in great haste' to be sung by the children from his Yorkshire village school as they marched to a neighbouring village in 1865. It was set to the music we know six years later by Arthur Sullivan, the well-known composer of operattas.

PRUNELLA SCALES

Actress

We used to sing 'Jerusalem' at school on Mondays – to start the week vigorously, I suppose – and it is of course the official hymn of the Labour Party. I love all Blake's writing – he was an extraordinarily original and radical spirit – and Parry's music seems to me to complement the poem to perfection. Having spent a good deal of my childhood among the 'dark satanic mills', I know a bit what it's about!

JERUSALEM

And did those feet in ancient time
Walk upon England's mountains green?
And was the Holy Lamb of God
On England's pleasant pastures seen?
And did the countenance divine
Shine forth upon our clouded hills?
And was Jerusalem builded here
Among these dark satanic mills?

Bring me my bow of burning gold!
Bring me my arrows of desire!
Bring me my spear! O clouds, unfold!
Bring me my chariot of fire!
I will not cease from mental fight,
Nor shall my sword sleep in my hand,
Till we have built Jerusalem
In England's green and pleasant land.

WILLIAM BLAKE (1757–1827)

MARJORIE SCARDINO

Businesswoman

I have been a closet hymn lover most of my life. Perhaps it's because church is where I learned to sing (not very well) and read music (not very well). So choosing a favourite hymn is almost impossible. It's a matter of occasion and mood. Pressed, I will follow my pantheistic tendencies and choose 'All Creatures Of Our God And King'. It has beautiful images from St Francis of Assisi, it carries the requisite and uplifting 'alleluyas' and it was beautifully arranged for the *New English Hymnal* by R Vaughan Williams.

ALL CREATURES OF OUR GOD AND KING

All creatures of our God and King,
lift up your voice and with us sing:
Hallelujah, hallelujah!
Thou burning sun with golden beam,
thou silver moon with softer gleam:
*O praise Him, O praise Him,
Hallelujah, hallelujah, hallelujah!*

Thou rushing wind that art so strong,
ye clouds that sail in heaven along,
O praise Him, hallelujah!
Thou rising morn, in praise rejoice,
ye lights of evening, find a voice:
O praise Him . . .

Thou flowing water, pure and clear,
make music for thy Lord to hear,
Hallelujah, hallelujah!
Thou fire so masterful and bright,
that givest man both warmth and light:
O praise Him . . .

And all ye men of tender heart,
forgiving others, take your part,
O sing ye, hallelujah!
Ye who long pain and sorrow bear,
praise God and on Him cast your care:
O praise Him . . .

Let all things their Creator bless,
and worship Him in humbleness,
O praise Him, hallelujah!
Praise, praise the Father,
praise the Son,
and praise the Spirit, Three-in-One:
O praise Him . . .

W H DRAPER (1855–1933)

SIR HARRY SECOMBE

Entertainer, Writer and Presenter

My favourite hymn and my mother's too is 'How Sweet The Name Of Jesus Sounds' by John Newton.

John Newton was a nasty piece of work in his younger days. He was a villain and a pirate. But he changed dramatically in his later years and wrote many more hymns. I found the words most moving at my mother's funeral.

HOW SWEET THE NAME OF JESUS SOUNDS

How sweet the name
of Jesus sounds
in a believer's ear!
It soothes his sorrows,
heals his wounds,
and drives away his fear.

It makes the wounded spirit whole,
and calms the troubled breast;
'tis manna to the hungry soul,
and to the weary rest.

Dear name! the rock on which I build,
my shield and hiding-place,
my never-failing treasury, filled
with boundless stores of grace.

Jesus! my shepherd, brother, friend,
my prophet, priest and king;
my lord, my life, my way, my end,
accept the praise I bring.

Weak is the effort of my heart,
and cold my warmest thought;
but when I see Thee as Thou art,
I'll praise Thee as I ought.

Till then I would Thy love proclaim
with every fleeting breath;
and may the music of Thy name
refresh my soul in death!

JOHN NEWTON (1725–1807)

MARIA SHAMMAS

Humanitarian

Despite the small fact that my Christian name is included in the title of this well-known hymn, I haven't chosen it for that reason. Instead, I've selected it for its striking capacity to express the greatest joy, and yet comfort during times of great pain and sorrow.

'Ave Maria' is in essence an exalted celebration, a tribute to the mother of Jesus. There's an amazing respect for and recognition of women in the four gospels. Jesus himself flouts the conventions of his time to bring women a previously unimagined status. Therefore for me the hymn is a celebration of women in general and motherhood in particular.

In another context the hymn carries with it echoes of mortality, because of war, disease, famine and natural disasters.

Most joyously, when the hymn is heard at weddings, it celebrates a sharing of love, commitment and unity before God. I value it for the reminder it gives us all of the need for compassion and humanity.

AVE MARIA

Ave Maria, gratia plena, Dominus tecum. Benedicta tu in mulieribus, et benedictus fructus ventris tui, Jesus. Sancta Maria, Mater Dei, ora pro nobis peccatoribus, nunc, et in hora mortis nos trae.
Amen.

Hail Mary, full of grace. The Lord is with thee. Blessed art thou among women, and blessed is the fruit of thy womb, Jesus. Holy Mary, Mother of God, pray for us sinners now, and at the hour of our death. Amen.

SALLY SHEINMAN

Artist

"'Kyrie Eleison', especially done in Gregorian chant, is very meaningful to me because the repetitive nature creates a tremendously peaceful atmosphere. As an artist who has just finished 2,000 paintings I feel that 'Kyrie Eleison' has truly helped me."

KYRIE ELEISON

Kyrie eleison, Christe eleison,
Kyrie eleison.

NED SHERRIN

Broadcaster and Writer

The first hymn I can remember is 'All Things Bright And Beautiful'. But it has to have the un-PC verse about:

The rich man in his castle,
the poor man at his gate,
He made them, high and lowly,
and order'd their estate.

ALL THINGS BRIGHT AND BEAUTIFUL

All things bright and beautiful,
all creatures great and small,
all things wise and wonderful,
the Lord God made them all.

Each little flower that opens,
each little bird that sings,
He made their glowing colours,
He made their tiny wings.
All things bright . . .

The purple-headed mountain,
the river running by,
the sunset, and the morning
that brightens up the sky;
All things bright . . .

The rich man in his castle,
the poor man at his gate,
He made them, high and lowly,
and order'd their estate.
All things bright . . .

The cold wind in the winter,
the pleasant summer sun,
the ripe fruits in the garden,
He made them every one.
All things bright . . .

He gave us eyes to see them,
and lips that we might tell
how great is God almighty,
who has made all things well.
All things bright . . .

C I ALEXANDER (1818–95)

JON SNOW

Journalist and Broadcaster

I had to sing 'He Who Would Valiant Be' to win a place in the Winchester Cathedral choir at seven years of age. It still summons up that glorious building, glimpses of the English countryside and childhood innocence. It embodies the essence of the Anglican Church threaded back through Byron to biblical times.

TO BE A PILGRIM

He who would valiant be
'gainst all disaster,
let him in constancy
follow the Master.
There's no discouragement
shall make him once relent,
his first avowed intent
to be a pilgrim.

Who so beset him round
with dismal stories,
so but themselves confound –
his strength the more is.
No foes shall stay his might,
though he with giants fight:
he will make good his right
to be a pilgrim.

Since, Lord, Thou dost defend
us with Thy Spirit,
we know we at the end
shall life inherit.
Then fancies flee away!
I'll fear not what men say,
I'll labour night and day
to be a pilgrim.

PERCY DEARMER (1867–1936)
AFTER JOHN BUNYAN (1628–88)

From *The English Hymnal* by permission of Oxford University Press.

RINGO STARR

Musician

'There Is A Green Hill Far Away' brings back fond memories of assembly at St Silas Primary School, Liverpool 8. I always loved the hymn, even though I suppose I was a little frightened at the time to hear that our Dear Lord was crucified – he died to save us all – but, nevertheless, ever since those childhood days it has been one of my favourites.

THERE IS A GREEN HILL FAR AWAY

There is a green hill far away,
without a city wall,
where the dear Lord was crucified,
who died to save us all.

We may not know, we cannot tell
what pains He had to bear;
but we believe it was for us
He hung and suffered there.

He died that we might be forgiven,
He died to make us good,
that we might go at last to heaven,
saved by His precious blood.

There was no other good enough
to pay the price of sin;
He only could unlock the gate
of heaven, and let us in.

Oh, dearly, dearly has He loved,
and we must love Him too;
and trust in His redeeming blood,
and try His works to do.

C F ALEXANDER (1818–95)

Horsley

WILLIAM HORSLEY (1774–1858)

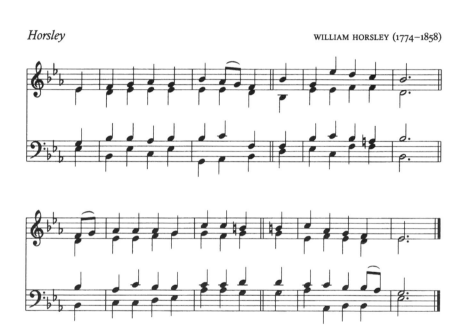

175

SIR SIGMUND STERNBERG

Businessman and Founder of the Three Faiths Forum

I have chosen 'The Divine Image' as it embodies the spirit which inspires the Interfaith work in which I have been so long engaged.

THE DIVINE IMAGE

To Mercy, Pity, Peace, and Love
All pray in their distress;
And to these virtues of delight
Return their thankfulness.

For Mercy, Pity, Peace, and Love
Is God, our father dear,
And Mercy, Pity, Peace, and Love,
Is Man, his child and care.

For Mercy has a human heart,
Pity a human face,
And Love, the human form divine,
And Peace, the human dress.

Then every man of every clime,
That prays in his distress,
Prays to the human form divine,
Love, Mercy, Pity, Peace.

And all must love the human form,
In heathen, turk, or jew;
Where Mercy, Love, and Pity dwell
There God is dwelling too.

BARONESS MARGARET THATCHER

Former Prime Minister

Although the great Hymns of Praise and their marvellous tunes crowd into one's mind immediately, I have chosen 'Jesus, Lover Of My Soul' sung to the tune 'Aberystwyth' because it concerns one's personal relationship with God, especially when times are difficult. Then these lovely words and this particular tune bring comfort and calm to the troubled mind.

JESUS, LOVER OF MY SOUL

Jesus, Lover of my soul,
Let me to thy bosom fly,
While the nearer waters roll,
While the tempest still is high;
Hide me, O my Saviour, hide,
Till the storm of life is past;
Safe into the haven guide,
O receive my soul at last!

Other refuge have I none;
Hangs my helpless soul on thee;
Leave, ah! Leave me not alone;
Still support and comfort me.
All my trust on thee is stayed;
All my help from thee I bring;
Cover my defenceless head
With the shadow of thy wing.

Thou, O Christ, art all I want;
More than all in thee I find;
Raise the fallen, cheer the faint,
Heal the sick, and lead the blind.
Just and holy is thy Name,
I am all unrighteousness;
False and full of sin I am,
Thou art full of truth and grace.

Plenteous grace with thee is found,
Grace to cover all my sin;
Let the healing streams abound;
Make and keep me pure within.
Thou of life the fountain art,
Freely let me take of thee;
Spring thou up within my hear,
Rise to all eternity.

CHARLES WESLEY (1707–88)

TOPOL

Singer and Actor

I sung Sheldon Harnick's Sabbath Prayer to Jerry Box's beautiful tune in more than 2,000 performances [of *Fiddler on the Roof*] over four continents.

I always felt the audience's awe when the candles were lit all over the stage, while the prayer was being sung. And, I have to admit, I too shared that same wonderful feeling with the audience.

THE SABBATH PRAYER

May the Lord protect and defend you.
May the Lord preserve you from pain.
Favour them, o Lord,
With happiness and peace.
O hear our Sabbath Prayer,
Amen.

SHELDON HARNICK

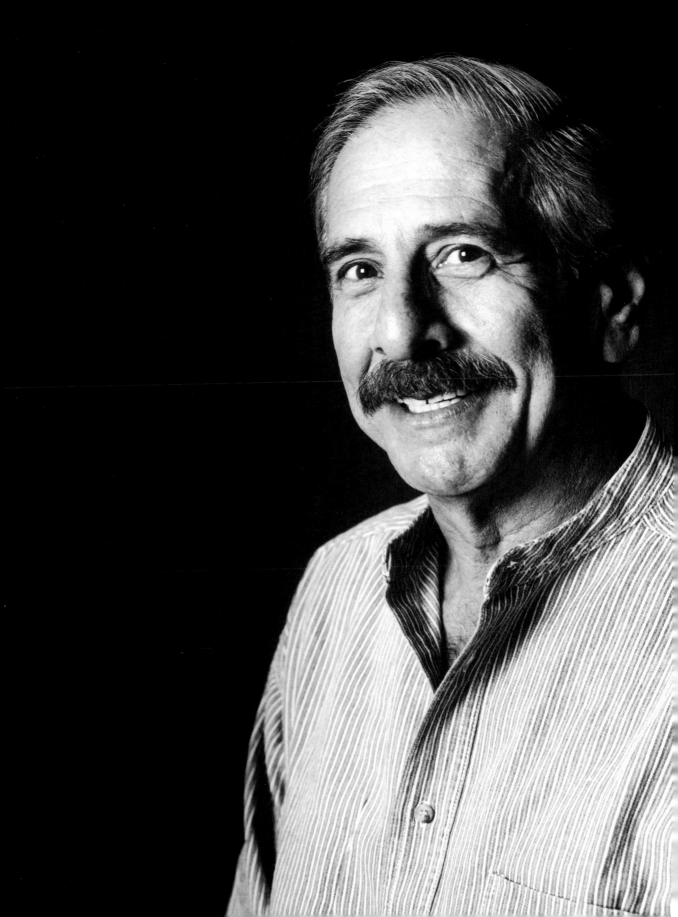

TERRY WAITE

Humanitarian

I like hymns for their tunes. As a chorister I sang my way through *Hymns Ancient and Modern* and later worked through *The English Hymnal*. For me the best tunes were found in the first book.

It's very difficult to choose one favourite. 'Lead Kindly Light', written by Newman in the Bay of Naples is certainly a moving tune and the words are not too bad. 'Lead Us Heavenly Father, Lead Us' is another stirring tune, as is 'Eternal Father, Strong To Save'.

However, if I were obliged to select one then it would be 'For all The Saints Who From Their Labours Rest'. This is a fine hymn for a procession and can be sung with great gusto.

FOR ALL THE SAINTS

For all the Saints
who from their labours rest,
who Thee by faith
before the world confessed,
Thy name, O Jesu, be for ever blest.
Alleluia!

Thou wast their Rock,
their fortress, and their might;
Thou, Lord, their Captain
in the well fought fight;
Thou in the darkness drear
their one true light.
Alleluia!

O may Thy soldiers,
faithful, true and bold,
fight as the Saints
who nobly fought of old,
and win, with them,
the victor's crown of gold!
Alleluia!

O blest communion, fellowship divine!
We feebly struggle, they in glory shine;
yet all are one in Thee,
for all are Thine.
Alleluia!

And when the strife is fierce,
the warfare long,
steals on the ear
the distant triumph song,
and hearts are brave again,
and arms are strong.
Alleluia!

WILLIAM WALSHAM HOW (1823–1897)

RICK WAKEMAN

Musician and Television Personality

To be able to look back over every day of our lives and to say thank you for the gift of life that each day brings is almost impossible to put into words. 'The Day Thou Gavest' somehow manages the impossible and is encased within one of the most beautiful melodies ever written.

THE DAY THOU GAVEST

The day Thou gavest, Lord, is ended,
The darkness falls at Thy behest;
To Thee our morning hymns ascended,
Thy praise shall sanctify our rest.

We thank Thee that Thy church unsleeping,
While earth rolls onward into light,
Through all the world her watch is keeping,
And rests not now by day or night.

As o'er each continent and island
The dawn leads on another day,
The voice of prayer is never silent,
Nor dies the strain of praise away.

The sun that bids us rest is waking
Our brethren 'neath the western sky,
And hour by hour fresh lips are making
Thy wondrous doings heard on high.

So be it, Lord; Thy throne shall never,
Like earth's proud empires, pass away;
Thy kingdom stands, and grows for ever,
Till all Thy creatures own Thy sway.

JOHN ELLERTON (1826–93)

CATHERINE WALKER

Fashion Designer

I was introduced to *The Prophet* by Kahlil Gibran by my late husband, and after his untimely death I drew strength from the following words, as I hope that many others will.

THEN A WOMAN SAID, SPEAK TO US

Then a woman said, Speak to us of Joy and Sorrow.
    And he answered:
    Your joy is in your sorrow unmasked
    And the selfsame well from which your laughter rises was oftentimes filled with your tears.
    And how else can it be?
The deeper that sorrow carves into your being, the more joy you can contain.
    Is not the cup that holds your wine the very cup that was burned in the potter's oven?
    And is not the lute that soothes your spirit the very wood that was hallowed with knives?
    When you are joyous, look deep into your heart and you shall find it is only that which has given you sorrow that is giving you joy.
    When you are sorrowful, look again in your heart, and you shall see that in truth you are weeping for that which has been your delight.
    Some of you say, 'Joy is greater than sorrow,' and others say, 'Nay, sorrow is the greater.'
    But I say unto you, they are inseparable.
    Together they come, and when one sits alone with you at your board, remember that the other is asleep upon your bed.
    Verily you are suspended like scales between your sorrow and your joy.
    Only when you are empty are you at standstill and balanced.
    When the treasure-keeper lifts you to weigh his gold and his silver, needs must your joy or your sorrow rise or fall.

EXTRACT FROM *THE PROPHET*

HARRIET WALTERS

Actress

When asked to name a favourite hymn nothing immediately came to mind, other than the rather overworked 'Dear Lord And Father Of Mankind' and 'Abide With Me' which I love more for the tunes than the words probably. Then, as I wandered about my business over the rest of the day, the words 'Immortal, Invisible . . .' and 'the ancient of days' and 'hid from our eyes' drifted up to the surface of my mind and I started to hum the tune. I saw a wide shaft of sunlight pouring in across a school assembly hall from a high up leaded window and rows of little girls in grey. Often I loved churning the words of hymns in my mouth without understanding their meaning necessarily. But 'invisible' is a more understandable God than the white-haired father figure we're supposed to know and love, and although I *still* don't really understand 'the ancient of days', it has a comfortingly abstract ring.

This hymn gives the mind room to wander. God can be what you want to believe He/She or It is.

IMMORTAL, INVISIBLE

Immortal, invisible, God only wise,
in light inaccessible hid from our eyes,
most blessed, most glorious,
the Ancient of Days,
almighty, victorious,
Thy great name we praise.

Unresting, unhasting,
and silent as light,
nor wanting, nor wasting,
Thou rulest in might;
Thy justice like mountains
high soaring above
Thy clouds, which are fountains
of goodness and love.

To all, life Thou givest,
to both great and small;
in all life Thou livest, the true life of all;
we blossom and flourish
as leaves on the tree,
and wither and perish,
but nought changeth Thee.

Immortal, invisible, God only wise,
in light inaccessible hid from our eyes,
most blessed, most glorious,
the Ancient of Days,
almighty, victorious,
Thy great name we praise.

W CHALMERS-SMITH (1824–1908)

A U B E R O N   W A U G H

Writer

"My favourite hymn was one I learned in my prep school – All Hallows, Cranmore, in Somerset – at the age of six. It was only ever sung in Catholic churches, which might have explained some of the passion with which it was sung, although, looking at it fifty years later, it seems to comprise nothing but disconnected, slightly incoherent exhortations. It doesn't even rhyme, but the tune is magnificent – I will sing it to you in private, if you like – and moved me profoundly when it was sung in raucous adolescent broken voices at Downside Abbey, where I attended public school. Hearing it sung in the parish church at home by women, I was particularly pleased by the thought of their sanctifying their breasts.

You seldom hear it nowadays. Like the Anglicans, the Catholics have sacked most of their grand old hymns, preferring sentimental modern rubbish with no tune to speak of. I think the reason for this is that the regular church attenders wish to discourage occasional visitors. It is a terrible shame."

SOUL OF MY SAVIOUR

Soul of my saviour, sanctify my breast,
body of Christ, be thou my saving guest,
blood of my saviour, bathe me in thy tide,
wash me with water flowing from thy side.

Strength and protection may thy passion be,
O blessed Jesu, hear and answer me;
deep in thy wounds, Lord, hide and shelter me,
so shall I never, never part from thee.

Guard and defend me from the foe malign,
in death's dread moments make me only thine;
call me and bid me come to thee on high
where I may praise thee with thy saints for ay.

LATIN, 14 CENTURY TRANS. ANON.

"'Love Divine' will remind us always of the most special day of our lives. (The hymn was the second at the marriage of Prince Edward to Sophie Rhys-Jones.)"

LOVE DIVINE

Love divine, all loves excelling,
joy of heaven, to earth come down:
fix in us Thy humble dwelling,
all Thy faithful mercies crown.
Jesus, Thou art all compassion,
pure, unbounded love Thou art;
visit us with Thy salvation,
enter every trembling heart.

Breathe, O breathe Thy loving Spirit
into every troubled breast;
let us all in Thee inherit,
let us find Thy promised rest.
Take away the love of sinning,
Alpha and Omega be;
end of faith, as its beginning,
set our hearts at liberty.

Come, almighty to deliver,
let us all Thy grace receive;
suddenly return, and never,
never more Thy temples leave.
Thee we would be always blessing,
serve Thee as Thy hosts above,
pray, and praise Thee without ceasing,
glory in Thy perfect love.

Finish then Thy new creation:
pure and spotless let us be;
let us see Thy great salvation,
perfectly restored in Thee:
Changed from glory into glory,
till in heaven we take our place,
till we cast our crowns before Thee,
lost in wonder, love, and praise.

CHARLES WESLEY (1707–88)

SIMON WESTON

Humanitarian

"I have chosen 'Myfanwy' because it is
Welsh, emotive and was sung at my
wedding by an Englishman who only had
a few weeks to learn it. It was sung so
well that ardent rugby players in the
congregation had tears in their eyes."

Paham mae digter, O! Myfanwy,
Yn llenwi'th lygaid duon di –
A'th ruddiau tirion, O! Myfanwy,
Heb wrido wrth fy ngweled i?
Pa le mae'r wen oedd ar dy wefus,
Fu'n cyneu cariad ffyddion ffol?
Pa le mae sain dy eiriau melus,
Fu'n denu nghalon ar dy ol?

Pa beth a wnaethum, O! Myfanwy,
I haeddu gwg dy ddwyndd hardd?
Ai chwareu'r oeddit, O! Myfanwy,
A thanau auraidd serch dy fardd?
Wyt eiddo i'm trwy gywit amod,
A'i gormod cadw'th air i mi?
Ni fynaf byth mo'th law, Myfanwy,
Heb gael dy galon gyda hi.

Myfanwy, boed yr oil o'th fywyd,
Dan heulwen ddisglaer canol dydd,
A boed i rosyn gwridog irchyd
I ddswnsio ganmlwydd ar dy rudd;
Anghofia'r oll o'th addwidion,
A wneist i rywun eneth ddel.
A dyro'th law, Myfanwy, dirion,
I ddim ond dweud gair – Ffarwl!

ANN WIDDECOMBE

MP

Very often people think that Christianity should guarantee a trouble-free life and that somehow it is the business of God to make everything turn out all right. In fact the lives of the early Apostles, Saints and Martyrs give us a very different picture. I have always believed that our business on this earth is to do our best, however difficult the circumstances, and that the courage to do so comes from God who then grants us eternal rest when we have finished with this life. This hymn sums up that approach.

FATHER, HEAR THE PRAYER WE OFFER

Father, hear the prayer we offer:
not for ease that prayer shall be,
but for strength, that we may ever
live our lives courageously.

Not for ever in green pastures
do we ask our way to be:
but by steep and rugged pathways
would we strive to climb to Thee.

Not for ever by still waters
would we idly quiet stay;
but would smite the living fountains
from the rocks along our way.

Be our strength in hours of weakness,
in our wanderings be our guide;
through endeavour, failure, danger,
Father, be Thou at our side.

Let our path be bright or dreary,
storm or sunshine be our share;
may our souls, in hope unweary,
make Thy work our ceaseless prayer.

MRS L M WILLIS (1824–1908)

LADY WILSON

Poet

I spent my childhood in a small village in East Anglia, where my father was minister of the congregational chapel. One particular Sunday comes to mind – it was the Sunday School Anniversary, and the boys were wearing white shirts and trousers, and the girls white dresses and straw hats. It was a beautiful summer day – the birds were singing outside, and the sun streamed through the windows.

I can see my father standing in the pulpit as we sang this hymn – a very happy memory.

SUMMER SUNS ARE GLOWING

Summer suns are glowing
Over land and sea,
Happy light is flowing
Bountiful and free;
Everything rejoices
In the mellow rays;
All earth's thousand voices
Swell the psalm of praise.

God's free mercy streameth
Over all the world,
And His banner gleameth
Everywhere unfurled;
Broad and deep and glorious
As the heaven above,
Shines in might victorious
His eternal Love.

Lord, upon our blindness
Thy pure radiance pour,
For Thy loving kindness
Make us love Thee more,
And when clouds are drifting
Dark across our sky,
Then, the veil uplifting,
Father, be Thou nigh.

We will never doubt Thee,
Though Thou veil Thy light;
Life is dark without Thee,
Death with Thee is bright,
Light of light, shine o'er us
On our pilgrim way,
Go Thou still before us
To the endless day.

WILLIAM WALSHAM HOW (1823–99)

NORMAN WISDOM

Comedy Actor and Television Personality

'Rock Of Ages' is my favourite hymn –
because we sang it at school.

ROCK OF AGES

Rock of ages, cleft for me,
let me hide myself in Thee;
let the water and the blood,
from Thy riven side which flowed,
be of sin the double cure,
cleanse me from its guilt and power.

Not the labour of my hands
can fulfil Thy law's demands;
could my zeal no respite know,
could my tears for ever flow,
all for sin could not atone;
Thou must save, and Thou alone.

Nothing in my hand I bring,
simply to Thy cross I cling;
naked, come to Thee for dress,
helpless, look to Thee for grace;
foul, I to the fountain fly;
wash me, Saviour, or I die.

While I draw this fleeting breath,
when mine eyes shall close in death,
when I soar through tracts unknown,
see Thee on Thy judgement throne;
Rock of ages, cleft for me,
let me hide myself in Thee.

AUGUSTUS M TOPLADY (1740–78)

KEVIN WOODFORD

Television Personality

"My favourite hymn is 'Abide With Me'. I always feel that it's like a spiritual version of being wrapped in a thick warm blanket on a cold evening."

ABIDE WITH ME

Abide with me;
fast falls the eventide;
the darkness deepens;
Lord, with me abide;
when other helpers fail,
and comforts flee,
help of the helpless, O abide with me.

Swift to its close
ebbs out life's little day;
earth's joys grown dim,
its glories pass away;
change and decay in all around I see:
O Thou who changest not,
abide with me!

I need Thy presence
every passing hour;
what but Thy grace
can foil the tempter's power?
Who like Thyself
my guide and stay can be?
Through cloud and sunshine,
O abide with me.

Hold Thou Thy cross
before my closing eyes,
shine through the gloom,
and point me to the skies;
heaven's morning breaks,
and earth's vain shadows flee:
in life, in death, O Lord, abide with me!

HENRY FRANCIS LYTE (1793–1847)

Eventide   W. H. MONK (1823–89)

SIR MAGDI YACOUB

Surgeon

"'Panis Angelicus' is my favourite hymn. It is very thoughtful; I like it."

PANIS ANGELICUS

Panis angelicus, fit panis hominum
Dat panis caelicus, figuris terminum.
Manducat Dominum,
Pauper, pauper, servus et humilis,
Pauper, pauper, servus et humilis.

Panis angelicus, fit panis hominum,
Dat panis caelicus figuris terminum.
O res mirabilis, manducat Dominum,
Pauper, pauper, servis et humilis.

Thus Angel's Bread is made
the Bread of man today;
the Living Bread from heaven
with figures dost away;
O wondrous gift indeed!
the poor and lowly may
upon their Lord and Master feed.
Thee, therefore, we implore,
O Godhead, One in Three,
so may Thou visit us
as we worship Thee;
and lead us on Thy way;
the light wherein Thou dwellest aye.

Copyright Acknowledgements

'To Be A Pilgrim'
Percy Dearmer (1867–1936) after
John Bunyan (1628–88)

'There Is A Green Hill Far Away'
Horsley

The Sabbath Prayer
Words by Sheldon Harnick

'Who Can Sound The Depths Of Sorrow'
Graham Kendrick (b. 1950)

'Zion Hort Die Wachter Singen'
(Zion Hears The Watchmen Calling) –
Bach's Cantata No. 10
Trans. Laurence Marks

Index to Contributors

Index to Hymn Choices